NEW TECHNOLOGY
FOR PROBLEM SOLVING

Three Disciplines for Systematic Innovation
in Business Information Technology

SCOTT WILGER

authorHOUSE®

AuthorHouse™
1663 Liberty Drive
Bloomington, IN 47403
www.authorhouse.com
Phone: 1 (800) 839-8640

Published by AuthorHouse   12/18/2015

ISBN: 978-1-5049-3300-1 (sc)
ISBN: 978-1-5049-3299-8 (e)

Library of Congress Control Number: 2015913511

Print information available on the last page.

CONTENTS

1.
THE BACK STORY

For some time starting in the mid-nineties, you could hardly pick up a book or article on IT project management that didn't reference the Standish Group's *CHAOS Manifesto*. It was almost as if an entire industry had a feeling that something was wrong, but no one could put their finger on it. And then there was the *CHAOS Manifesto*, which put a name to our pain. It told us that on average, nearly 85 percent of all IT projects fail, and it told us why. And everyone said "I knew it! Everyone else really does suck!"

Year after year the Standish Group published the *CHAOS Manifesto* and year after year nothing changed. Book after book was written, each one describing exactly what the problems were and how to solve them. There were books on risk management, software development methodologies, project management techniques, Eastern religion (not kidding: *Zen and the Art of Systems Analysis*) — you name it. Project managers blamed insufficient project management controls, inadequate techniques, inexperienced and insufficiently skilled project managers, and insufficiently skilled team members. Business analysts blamed poorly defined requirements, clients who didn't know what they wanted, and developers who ignored requirements or who were not skilled enough to properly translate them into software. Business people complained about how their internal IT organizations and consultants were under-skilled, didn't understand the nuances of the business, didn't listen, and took *forever* to get anything done. Developers complained about incomplete requirements, business analysts who couldn't define requirements that could be translated to design, and business customers who were clueless. Generally, the most common reasons for project failure could be boiled down to insufficiently skilled practitioners, inadequate processes and controls, poorly defined and incomplete requirements, inadequate executive support, insufficient testing, and the rapid pace of change in both technology and the business environment in general. Prescribed solutions ran the gamut: more controls, fewer controls, more rigorous processes, less rigorous processes, more sophisticated contractual arrangements and fee structures, better, smarter, faster people.

In the 20 years since *The Chaos Manifesto* was first published, what was once all the buzz, hardly anyone remembers. A whole generation of leaders has been replaced by a new class. Absolutely nothing has changed, except to get somewhat worse, if that's possible. Everyone still complains about the same problems, but it seems as if a chronic state of dysfunction has simply become the expectation.

Sadly, for at least the last decade, the popular focus of IT leadership has been almost exclusively on reducing cost per hour, the least important of all factors related to performance. Worse, this obsession with cost per hour has had the unintended and largely unacknowledged side effect of dramatically eroding the most important factor of all: *productivity.*

Many of the standard "best" practices that we continue to apply, particularly in the area of project management, are left over from an era when productivity depended entirely on leveraging labor — managing tasks and time. But in our current knowledge-based economy,[1] the creation of value depends primarily on *creativity and innovation*. We aren't shoveling sand. We are *inventing* new things.

Equally troubling and less obvious are the patterns of behavior that consistently torpedo our efforts. They are insidious and deeply entrenched, not only in the way we approach IT projects, but also in the way we approach leadership, management, and interpersonal relationships in the business context. Big advances have been made in systems implementation methodologies, tools, and techniques, and they have certainly been of tremendous value. There is always room for improvement when it comes to the mechanics of systems implementation, but by and large, they do nothing to change behaviors. While the behaviors remain the same, the results will not change.

When we manage to change these behaviors and turn our attention to productivity, the results are remarkable. It turns out that complex systems implementation efforts are not required to be chaotic, painful, contentious, and draining. They are not required to have a high probability of failure. We are not required to chew through people, use them up, and burn them out. It is not necessary to operate in a continuous state of crisis. It is not required that businesses suffer enormous economic loss in the process. When all factors come together into that magical combination where everything clicks, this work is highly successful and deeply rewarding.

The productivity gains are even more remarkable. My team and I have been doing this kind of work, together and separately, for quite some time. By comparing our own results over time, comparing our results to other teams on similar work (and in two instances on the *same work*), and by comparing the results of new team members before and after they have adopted our disciplines, we are finding that we are *at least* two to four times more productive than our peers.

Think about that: on comparable work, a team of three of our people can do the work of 6 to 12 people. On large projects, we consistently outpace the rest of the project team by months, even when our portions of the projects are enormously complex. The projects or portions of projects that we control are almost always successful, even when the rest of the project is deeply troubled. Since productivity and quality go hand-in-hand, the solutions we build are of very high quality. We experience fewer defects, fewer missed requirements, and fewer misinterpreted requirements. Our solutions are highly maintainable and enhanceable for years to come. Most importantly, they consistently achieve their stated objectives, adding real value to our customers' businesses.

Not surprisingly, our customers are very happy. We tend to build very strong and lasting relationships with them. Many have become friends. We often work together for years. From a consulting perspective, the work is more fun, less stressful, and far more rewarding.

These kinds of results are not achieved by chance. They come at a price, and that price is *relentless, uncompromising discipline.* The fact is that it is hard. Everything we do to achieve these results is interconnected and mutually reinforcing. This means that it's not an option to choose to do "just a little." You either do this, or you don't. There is no in-between.

Does this mean that we have become immune to failure? Unfortunately, no. On any given project, only so many factors fall within our scope of control and influence. No amount of sophistication at executing IT projects will overcome systemic organizational weaknesses such as fundamental leadership issues, lack of vision, or paralyzing politics. But what we can do, and in fact are obligated to do, is to learn to be more successful within our scope of control and influence. As we experience more success, our scope of control will expand, and over time, we can have an ever-larger impact on success overall. An important common denominator is like-minded people: people who are devoted to something larger than themselves, who are hungry for a better way, who are open to trying something new, and who are fearless in the pursuit. We are looking for those people.

Notes

1.   Drucker, Peter F. Post-Capitalist Society. New York: Routledge, 2011. iBooks. https://itun.es/us/LRBnH.l. p. 14.

2.
OPENING THOUGHTS

New Technology for Problem Solving: *The component technologies, or disciplines, required to successfully accomplish complex transformations of business systems.*

Technology: *"If a learning organization were an engineering innovation, such as the airplane or the personal computer, the components would be referred to as "technologies." For an innovation in human behavior, the components need to be seen as disciplines."*

PETER M. SENGE [1]

Discipline: *"...a body of theory and technique that must be studied and mastered to be put into practice."*

PETER M. SENGE [2]

Advances in technology continue to present companies with new opportunities for growth as well as new competitive threats. For example, internet and mobile technologies introduced vast new possibilities for companies to engage and serve their customers in entirely new ways, as well as to develop entirely new products and services, in other words, to dramatically change and enhance their value propositions to their customers. The advancements in technology and the possibilities that have emerged as a result, have compelled companies to *transform* their value chain processes in order to avail themselves of these possibilities as well as to respond to new competitive threats. These might be modest transformations, but very often, they are significant.

For example, a large retailer whose value chain is traditionally geared toward physical retail locations faces a significant effort to extend its shopping experience online to its customers. The online storefront itself is only moderately complex technically. The real complexity is more subtle, and arises as the company attempts to extend its brand and shopping experience to an entirely new medium. Behind the scenes, the supply chain is very different, placing new demands on inventory management, supplier relationships, and order fulfillment. If the company has any uniqueness in its value chain that provides it with a distinct competitive advantage, this uniqueness must be respected and extended to the new channel. These are serious challenges. How does the company extend its value proposition in ways that enhance and complement what the company *already is*, that which is already compelling to its customers and provides it with a defendable market position? [3]

It's not the same as implementing a new accounting system or email system, that's for sure. Implementing the technology itself is not that difficult. Pure technology endeavors, such as implementing complex networks or other infrastructure efforts, are much like constructing buildings. They involve detail complexity, with lots of steps and moving parts, and they are well suited to traditional project management and oversight. It's not to say that they are always easy, or that they don't have their problems. However, they are largely successful, and we rarely hear of projects of this nature failing. I never once saw a headline that read "Company Fails Miserably at

Implementing Word Processing on its Desktops!" Where we tend to fail is at executing complex transformational efforts.

Transformational efforts are different. They involve not only detail complexity, but dynamic complexity. Peter Senge describes dynamic complexity as "situations where cause and effect are subtle, and where the effects over time of interventions are not obvious." Problems are dynamically complex when "the same action has dramatically different effects in the short run and the long," and "when an action has one set of consequences locally and a very different set of consequences in another part of the system."[4] Transformational efforts in a business setting are dynamically complex if only for the fact that business organizations themselves are dynamically complex. Transformational efforts require a willingness and ability to view the organization as a system. They require a strong element of *creativity* and problem solving, the courage to change everything, and the ability to *invent* whatever is required to accomplish the transformation. They suffer at the hands of traditional, linear, command and control project management. A transformational effort may be large. Implementing a new Enterprise Resource Planning (ERP) system involves a company's entire supply chain and many of its support functions. Or it may be relatively small, such as implementing an online store front. But they are both transformational efforts none-the-less, and subject to a different set of rules and requirements.

We tend to view transformational efforts as technology efforts, but technology is merely an enabler. For example, a new product launch is a transformational effort by any measure. It involves product design and marketing. It affects the supply chain, manufacturing, and distribution. It will almost certainly involve technology. These days, any transformational effort likely will. But technology is only one aspect of the effort. It no more defines the product launch, or *is* the product launch, than concrete *is* the foundation of a building. Information technology is only a building material.

The fact is that transformational efforts, by nature, are difficult. It is notable that product launches fail at a similar rate to complex IT endeavors. So what really separates a successful effort from one that fails? Why is one project team successful, and another not?

It turns out that the single most important characteristic that a project team must possess in order to successfully execute transformational efforts is not among those most commonly cited, and it certainly has nothing to do with the cost per hour of labor: *it is the ability to learn, create, and innovate as a team.* Furthermore, to be consistently successful, that ability has to be systematic. By systematic, I mean deliberate, repeatable, and predictable.

Experience Is Helpful, But...

Experience within a particular problem domain or within a particular industry can be useful, but in actuality, it is not critical. All businesses, even businesses within the same industry, are different, and usually vastly different. This is a natural condition created by the forces of competition. Businesses are driven to differentiate themselves in order to defend their competitive positions. They differentiate not only on product features and price, but also on what they do and how they do it. This means that regardless of how many years you have spent in a particular industry or how many complex systems you have implemented, every situation you encounter and every problem you face will be unique. Experience may make us feel comfortable, but it is limited in its ability to inform us as to *what we need to create or invent in order to solve the problem at hand.* Over-reliance on and misplaced faith in experience can actually contribute to failure, since it often inhibits inquisitiveness and the free exchange of ideas. The only experience that really matters is experience in the activity of *deliberate creativity and innovation.*

Project Management Expertise Is Critical, But...

Strong project management processes and skills are certainly critical to the success of any effort. But project management is not the single most important factor for success for one simple reason: project management does nothing to inform us as to *what we need to create or invent in order to solve the problem at hand*. Project management helps us understand the steps we need to take, in what order. It helps us understand timeframes, interdependencies, and costs. It allows us to track our progress, and helps us to understand the corrective actions we might take if we fall behind. Project management does not create solutions, it informs the process of implementing them.

Our traditional project management techniques are a large contributor to our problems. These techniques, developed over the last 150 years, are well suited to managing tasks and labor. They work well when the desired outcome is well known and the tasks to achieve that outcome are discrete and well defined. For example, they work well for construction projects and IT infrastructure projects. They work well when a detailed design with a high degree of fidelity can be reliably produced within a reasonable amount of time prior to starting, and where there is little risk of major changes in conditions or requirements during that time. This is certainly not the case for transformational efforts in a business setting. These techniques were originally developed when the productivity of labor was the key concern. Labor was a commodity, and productivity was less a matter of skill than it was of management. But for transformational efforts, it is the productivity of *knowledge* that matters. Furthermore, knowledge is never a commodity. You simply cannot effectively apply the same management principles to the application of knowledge that you do to the application of a shovel to dirt.

Skilled Team Members Are Important, But...

There is no question that skilled, competent team members are a requirement for project success. Yet countless project teams, filled with highly skilled and dedicated team members, have failed. W. Edwards Deming wrote,

> "Suppose that (1) everybody knew what to do. (2) Everybody did his best. Result: dissipation of knowledge and effort; results, far from optimum."[5]

We always seem to think we know what to do. And the majority of people the majority of the time work very hard and put forth their best efforts. But individuals, no matter how skilled, will fail if they are unable as a team *to create and invent what they need in order to solve the problem at hand*. The key words here are *as a team*. In an industry where individual skill and prowess are highly prized, ego and personal ambition tend to inhibit collaborative creativity. We are often too busy trying to convince each other how smart we are to make time to listen to each other and work together in order to create something truly valuable. We are often too busy defending our own ideas to develop a common understanding and shared vision. Furthermore, the skills we value so highly pale in comparison to the value of raw creativity, a trait rarely, if every mentioned, much less specifically cultivated, in the IT industry.

Executive Support Is Important, But...

Executive support is often cited as a critical factor for project success. Without a doubt, a project without executive support will fail, if for no other reason than the problem at hand does not adequately capture the imaginations and attentions of the decision makers. But no amount of executive commitment is enough if they don't know what they have committed *to*. It's not enough for executive sponsors to say that they are committed, to sit through a project status meeting once a week, and sign funding requests. The decision makers must be willing and able to participate in the process of determining *what they need to create or invent in order to solve the problem at hand*. If they are not part of the process of invention, their own mental models will almost certainly conflict with the solution created. Without the benefit of participating in the creative process, they simply won't understand, and will likely impede the successful implementation of the solution.

There Is No 'Recipe' for Success

Businesses are complex and unique. The business problems that we face are complex and unique. Nothing happens the same way twice. No two problems, or solutions to solve them, are alike. If you are out there long enough, either as a consultant or as a business leader, you will eventually find yourself facing problems that are beyond your depth. No amount of experience, individual skill, project management, or executive support is enough in the face of overwhelming uncertainty and complexity, so our ability to successfully implement solutions to complex problems depends foremost on our ability to learn, create, and innovate predictably and repeatably. This ability has to be cultivated. It requires personal commitment, sustained effort, and discipline: three disciplines actually, a discipline of clarity, a discipline of process, and a discipline of trust.

Notes

1. Senge, Peter M. *The Fifth Discipline: The Art and Practice of the Learning Organization*. Rev. and updated ed. New York: Doubleday/Currency, 2006. p. 10

2. ibid.

3. For an excellent real-life example of this exact challenge, search the Internet for Target Corp and e-commerce between 2013 and 2014.

4. ibid. 1, p. 71-72

5. Deming, W. Edwards. *Out of the Crisis*. Cambridge, Mass.: Massachusetts Institute of Technology, Center for Advanced Engineering Study, 1986. p.19

PART 1:
THE DISCIPLINE OF TRUST

I begin with the discipline of trust because it is the foundation on which everything else rests. It is also the most difficult for people to accept and certainly the most difficult to adopt. It tends to make people uncomfortable. The concepts seem too "touchy-feely," too soft for the tough and practical world of business. They seem out of place in the science-like field of information technology. If this proves true for you, here is something to keep in mind: in the application of text-critical analysis to the study of the Bible, one of the criteria applied for determining the more reliable of two conflicting versions of the same text is that the more *difficult* reading is probably the more reliable one (i.e., the "oldest and best"). What textual critics have discovered is to pay close attention when they come across an interpretation that makes them uncomfortable because it is theologically problematic. They have learned to dig deeper rather than dismiss it out of hand. I would encourage you to do the same as I make my case for trust.

In a team situation, without trust among people, there can be no innovation. Learning, creativity, and innovation are severely impaired or completely non-existent in environments that are low in trust and high in fear. People become consumed with self-preservation. Fear and distrust cause people to keep their heads down and measure their words. And the moment we begin to measure our words, when we become unwilling to challenge each other's assumptions, or when we withhold our own opinions and ideas, the game is lost. A discipline of trust is more than simply saying "I trust you." It is a commitment to building trust along the way — in how we choose to do things and in the ways that we interact. Unfortunately, when it comes to building relationships and trust, we have been dealt a pretty weak hand to begin with.

3.

THE PROFESSIONAL PARADOX

In the early 1980s, Donald Schön in his book, *The Reflective Practitioner* described a "crisis of confidence" in the professions, such as medicine, engineering, business management, and politics "rooted both in their perceived failure to live up to their own norms, and in their perceived incapacity to help society achieve its objectives and solve its problems."[1] He described an erosion in the perceived legitimacy of the professions starting from their peak in the 1960s when they were held in the absolute highest regard and trust, to a deep questioning "of the professionals' claim to extraordinary knowledge in matters of human importance."[2] Schön cited a series of national crises between 1963 and 1982, including the Vietnam War, deteriorating cities, poverty, the pollution of the environment, and the energy crisis that "seemed to have roots in the very practices of science, technology, and public policy called upon to alleviate them."[3] The solutions to major problems that were conceived by professionals turned out to be "ineffective," caused "new problems," or were "derived from theories shown to be fragile and incomplete."[4] Scandals involving Medicare and Medicaid, and Watergate and its aftermath, further tarnished the public image of the professions.

It would appear that the crisis of confidence that he described was only the beginning of a long decline. One crisis or scandal after another has beset us: Michael Milken and junk bonds in the 1980s, the savings and loan crisis in the 1990s, the ongoing and deepening healthcare crisis, and the lunacy of the dot com bubble. Our confidence in the professions and related institutions continues to erode. This is not surprising in light of events such as Enron, the evaporating "evidence" that led us into the Iraq War, and the almost unfathomable greed and incompetence within the financial industry and the federal government that resulted in the crushing financial crisis that affected the entire world in 2008. Schön wrote in 1982 that, "Apparently, professionals could not be counted on to police themselves, to live to the standards of probity, which set them above the ethical level of the general public. Like everyone else, they seemed ready to put their special status to private use."[5] Today, that would be considered a given. Incompetence is generally assumed, not to mention a strong disposition to believe in outright criminal intent. The increasingly contentious, polarized, and strident nature of our political system is symptomatic of our eroding confidence and loss of trust.

I am not old enough to remember a time when professionals enjoyed any sort of public admiration or "special status" as described by Schön. Over the course of my life and my career, skepticism and distrust of professionals and professional institutions has only deepened. The IT consulting profession certainly enjoys no better status. "Consulting" is almost a dirty word, and the profession is viewed with open scorn. There are three types of people, the saying goes: those who can, those who can't and teach, and those who *really* can't and consult.

The paradox is that even though we believe consultants are basically clowns and con men, when faced with a complex problem, one of the first things that we do is seek out "experts" who can help — professional consultants or consulting companies. Despite the fact that we really don't think much of consultants in general, and certainly don't trust them, this is one of the primary ways in which we attempt to deal with complexity and uncertainty. It seems logical — find a person or an organization who has been down this road before and who can show us the way. In theory, these experts know something we don't. They have already dealt with the messiness of it all, they are wise to what lies ahead, and therefore, the complexity and uncertainty will be minimized.

There is nothing wrong with asking for help. In fact, it is an absolute necessity because none of us possess the specialized knowledge and skills required to tackle every situation that confronts us. Whether in business or in our personal lives, it is simply a reality that we frequently require the services of professionals who specialize in a field of knowledge or skill. It is this reality that provides us with so many opportunities to choose our dance partners and step out onto the floor, sometimes successfully, sometimes not.

Within the realm of IT consulting, and probably in any business or personal context in which we deal with consultants, there are three primary factors that contribute to the ultimate destruction of the client-consultant relationship. The problems start because when we look for help, we approach it the wrong way and ask for the wrong things. They are exacerbated by the escalation of distrust resulting from our deep-seated fear associated with financial concerns. Finally, they are made insurmountable by the further escalation of distrust resulting from the bad behavior which is generally accepted and even encouraged in our business environment today. The discipline of trust explores how we, as consultants and clients, can learn to recognize these factors, take the appropriate steps to mitigate them, and unleash the power of truly collaborative relationships that will fundamentally change our outcomes.

Notes

1.   Schön, Donald A. *The Reflective Practitioner: How Professionals Think in Action*. New York: Basic Books, 1983. p. 39

2.   ibid. p. 5

3.   ibid. p. 9

4.   ibid. p. 10

5.   ibid. p. 11

4.

THE ENEMIES OF TRUST

F ear is the ultimate enemy of trust. Whether it is the fear of failure, financial fear, or the fear of how you are perceived in a business setting, it is fear that destroys trust above all else. In the business setting, it manifests in some predictable ways.

THE CLIENT EXPECTATION
AND THE CONSULTING VALUE PROPOSITION

If you are a business person in search of help, probably one of the first things you will do is write a request for proposal (RFP) or a request for service (RFS). You may even hire a consultant to help you do this. In this process, you figure that if experience is good then more experience must be better. You probably place a strong emphasis on experience in your industry, experience with a particular type of problem, with a particular software application, with projects just like yours, and years of experience overall. And then you begin to think of it as a numbers game. Considering the shear volume of people who are likely to see your RFP or RFS, why not set the bar high? Surely there must be many people out there with the depth and breadth of experience and skills to fully encompass your needs. So for good measure, you sprinkle in such things as project management expertise, knowledge of a specific technology or architecture, strong analytical skills, and leadership ability. By the time you are finished, you may as well be asking for a guy who walks on water and can feed the masses with a handful of fish and a few loaves of bread.

Amazingly, most of the consultants and consulting companies who respond appear to be exactly what you are looking for. There are a few odd ones who emphasize problem solving processes and their track records in addressing complex issues, but their examples aren't specific to your industry, and they didn't seem to focus on the specific skill sets that you asked for. You reject them immediately. You interview a number of respondents. Some of them are actual consultants, and some of them are sales people for consulting companies. Some that looked great on paper turned out to be total goof balls. This might make you a little uneasy, but eventually you find a consultant or a company that seems right.

Having made your selection, the consultant (or team of consultants) shows up at your site to begin working with you and your team. You made it clear in the selection process that you were looking for Superman. The consultant, having no real benchmark for comparison, believes that you know better than he does the skill sets and experience levels that actually exist in the consulting marketplace. Yet somehow, you picked him. He knows that he isn't Superman, but he's up to the challenge. In this first contact with you, he feels tremendous pressure to meet your expectations. His first priority is to convince you that he is all that, and that he in fact, does have all the answers.

Nothing irritates customers more than consultants who think they have all the answers. So from the outset, you are off to a shaky start. The team's initial perception is that the consultant is arrogant and self-important. This perception is reinforced as the consultant offers up vignettes of experience and expertise that are painfully inappropriate to your particular context because he isn't listening, and he is making assumptions about your needs based on what he has learned from other engagements. The team is compelled to enlighten him. You now enter a downward spiral: 1) You asked for Superman; 2) The consultant tries to convince you that he is Superman; 3) You try to convince him that he is not; 4) He senses danger and tries even harder; 5) You respond in turn. The process finally ends when you become very irritated and try to make it abundantly clear that he doesn't know @#$! about your company or your problems and that he needs to shut up and listen!

This may be an extreme example to make my point, but many engagements begin with some form of this scenario. It is basically built in to the existing structure of the client expectation and the consulting value proposition. Consumers of consulting services express a need that emphasizes depth of experience and specialized skills centered specifically around their particular industries, problem types, and anticipated technology needs. This is what consultants and consulting companies perceive as the market need, and so they respond accordingly. Individual consultants are driven to specialize in a particular industry, and further in a particular type of problem within the industry. They focus on developing skills with a particular tool or set of tools. Consulting companies are driven to be all things to all people. They attempt to hire and maintain a stable of consultants to satisfy every possible need. To increase the breadth of their markets and their economic potential, they try to hire individuals with experience in different industries and skills in particular technologies. They must present themselves as the experts with all the answers, because that is what the market demands.

This structure on its surface seems only natural, and hardly a threat. But it leads to a more serious and insidious problem. Remember that the professional consultant fears complexity for the same reasons as everyone else: complexity means uncertainty; uncertainty means risk of failure; failure may be career-ending.

As Schön put it, "For [professionals], uncertainty is a threat; its admission is a sign of weakness."[1] This is compounded by the perception, real or imagined, that the consulting value proposition rests on being the specialist and having all the answers. Consultants have invested heavily financially, intellectually, and emotionally in their particular marketable basket of skills, experiences, and tools which they *need to believe* will allow them to tackle any situation they may come across. They are strongly incentivized to make problems fit within their particular scope of skills and experience. Their economic survival depends on it.

Schön described this tendency in professionals as "cutting the practice situation to fit professional knowledge." He identified a number of ways that professionals "misread situations, or manipulate them," which amount to ignoring or explaining away aspects of problem situations that don't work for them. One is "selective inattention" to details that are problematic. Another is the use of "junk categories" to dismiss details or outcomes that they otherwise could not explain. Forcing a situation into a mold, or over-simplifying it to fit a particular solution pattern or tool set, is a very common approach in the IT consulting world.[2] In the end, your consultants may not be solving your problem at all, but some version of your problem that fits nicely within their professional spectrums.

Besides trying to preserve our own appearances as experts, this is another example of one of the primary, and ineffective, ways that we deal with complexity and uncertainty. Uniqueness makes us uncomfortable because it defies patterns of understanding. Information or conditions that are new or puzzling threaten us. Some of the techniques that are used in the field of IT to eliminate uniqueness and ignore complexity are so common and entrenched that they are actually accepted as best practices.

I witnessed an interesting example of this while working for a major systems integrator on a large project for one of the largest public housing authorities in the nation. The intent of the project was to replace the client's outdated and inadequate supply chain systems. It was a worthy effort, with the intention of dramatically improving the customer experience while significantly improving productivity and lowering costs. The primary platform of choice was a well known Customer Relationship Management (CRM) application. The systems integrator had deployed a team of people who belonged to a practice group that specialized in implementing this particular application. These people, including project managers, team leads, business analysts, technical architects, and developers, were, in theory, well-trained on the application and had experience implementing it one or more times in similar situations.

I was engaged during the requirements definition phase of the project to help define the requirements and business rules around certain aspects of the business such as determining if applicants were eligible for public housing and scheduling applicant interviews. Being new to the project, the first thing I needed was some context regarding the business processes that included these activities and information regarding the decision processes that they contained. A group of business analysts had been working to define these processes for several months. To get up to speed, I began by reviewing the processes that they had defined.

I quickly discovered that I could not decipher them on my own. I scheduled meetings with the analysts who authored the process definitions so that we could review them together. Even then, I struggled to understand them. Keep in mind that I was not new to the discipline of business process definition. I admit that I am no rocket scientist, but I can assure you that it was not rocket science. When a highly-experienced business analyst cannot quickly come up to speed by reviewing the work of other analysts, something is wrong.

When we began to review these business processes, I found that they had defined them entirely in terms of the functionality within the CRM application. They had literally defined process steps according to screens and other functionality that they believed should be invoked to execute the business processes. Understand that we were in the requirements definition phase, not the design phase. The analysts had defined the business processes entirely in terms of what they believed the CRM application could do.

This was problematic for a number of reasons. First, they had limited the requirements of the business processes by trying to answer the question of *what* the business needed to do in terms of *how* it could be done with the functionality available within the application. Second, they had further limited the requirements to fit *their* understanding of what the application could do. Finally, they had actually defined process tasks in terms of the CRM application's lexicon rather than the lexicon of the business.

The resulting business process definitions were shallow and incomplete, made little sense in the context of what the business actually did, and were defined in a language that could not be understood unless you were well versed in the application itself. As a result, the business processes were virtually indecipherable to a business person or to someone new to the project. By all measures, the team was "cutting the practice situation to fit their professional knowledge." They scoped the problem to fit the tools at hand. They further scoped it to fit within their incomplete knowledge of the tools. And finally, they defined the requirements for the solution in a language that only they understood. Most troubling of all is that this was considered an acceptable and appropriate practice. In fact, when aspects of the problem situation were identified that did not fit well within the limits of the application, the team was encouraged to either alter the requirements to make them fit, or to formally identify them as out of scope. The business analysts were doing exactly what they were trained to do, according to established and accepted "best practices."

The resulting client-consultant relationship could not be a better example to make my point. The tension between the consultants and the business people had become so great that when I arrived I wasn't even allowed to contact the business stakeholders directly. All of my questions had to be presented to the client in writing by a business analyst on the project team, after being carefully screened. When I was eventually able to convince people that I could actually handle myself in front of the client, I was subjected to intense coaching, and provided such valuable insights as "don't say 'Um' too much," and "don't touch the projector screen while you're presenting, it makes Jane really mad." Every meeting had to be arduously documented and the meeting notes routed through several layers of approval. I have never seen a group of consultants so terrified of their customers, or a group of business stakeholders so angry with their consultants.

The impact on productivity was profound. With no adequate context for dealing with complexity, low trust, and tremendous levels of fear, minor project questions that should have been resolvable within the scope of hour-long meetings required days or even weeks to fully resolve. When decisions were finally made, they were often poorly thought out and shallow. As one might expect, the project was continually behind schedule and over budget, which only served to further fuel the distrust and fear, and tighten the downward spiral.

This tendency is not exclusive to the consulting side of the relationship. Clients also fear complexity, and have their own ways of "cutting the practice situation." For example, clients tend to resist the notion that their problems are truly unique. It is a paradox in itself: from a competitive point of view, they want to be unique, but operationally they would rather be the same. The problem is, you can't have both. Competitive differentiation is not simply a matter of *what you say* makes you unique. It actually manifests from *what you do*. But uniqueness defies "patterns" of understanding, and in the business world, this tends to make people very uncomfortable. Business people love patterns. Patterns can be studied, learned, and applied. Clients tend to be obsessive about "best practices," finding pre-built solutions that meet "eighty percent of our needs," and then fiercely resisting attempts to customize the pre-built solution to meet their remaining 20 percent.

Between clients and practitioners, we have created a cycle that reinforces our low opinions of of each other, fuels distrust, inhibits our ability to solve problems and increases our odds of failure: 1) Customers experience project failures; 2) They respond by demanding more specialized expertise and experience; 3) Consultants respond by becoming increasingly specialized; 4) Consultants (and clients) are deeply incentivized to force problems into their patterns of specialized understanding; 5) Solutions are awkward, narrowly and poorly defined, or simply make no sense relative to the problem at hand; 6) Customers experience project failures. And the spiral continues.

FINANCIAL MATTERS

And then there is money. On a day-to-day basis, there is nothing in our personal or professional lives that can provoke a fear response quite like money. Specifically, spending too much of it, wasting it, or running out of it. Within the dynamics of the client-consultant relationship, financial considerations and the fear associated with them are profoundly influential. Without a doubt, it is the financial aspects of projects that fuel the acrimony in the client-consultant relationship to the highest degree.

In today's consulting environment, the going-in position for the client is that your consultants are going to try to rob you. The reality of your project will be quite different from the picture painted for you during the sales process. The enthusiasm to help and the concern for your success demonstrated during the sales process is disingenuous window-dressing. Initial project cost and time estimates are works of fiction, with no basis in reality, made to be what they had to be to make the sale. The shamelessly obvious goal of the consulting organization is to extract as much money as possible from you in the form of billable hours and reimbursable expenses. The seemingly smart and talented people you began working with, and with whom you have started building relationships, will not be the people who actually show up to work on your project. The consultants that work on your project will be ridiculously under-skilled and over-priced. They will have no clue how to actually pull off what they have been assigned to do. They will have no formal methods, processes, or tools. Everything they do they will make up as they go. Consultants are basically incompetent, lying, cheating thieves.

Conversely, if you are a consultant, your going-in position is that the client always wants something for nothing. Their shamelessly obvious objective is to make sure that you don't make a dime on their project. They tear out their hair and feign shock at project cost and time estimates. They will do everything they can to beat down your numbers. They will swoon at your rates. They will question every time estimate for every task. They will grudgingly, even angrily trim scope and "lower their expectations" in order to get to a number and a time frame that they can accept. Throughout the project, they will do everything in their power to add back their original scope (and then some), while acting incensed at the suggestion that the project budget would have to increase. They will threaten you. They will bully you. They will withhold payment.

Without a doubt, there is ample experience and evidence on both sides of the fence to prove that we are both right. But once again, we are creating our own reality. In his book, *The Fifth Discipline*, Peter M. Senge identifies recurring systemic patterns, which he calls system archetypes, that control events.[3] These are patterns that occur over and over, and of which we are generally unaware. Among them is a pattern he calls "Shifting the Burden." This pattern occurs when an underlying problem exists that is difficult to address. The difficulty may arise for any number of reasons, including complexity, obscurity, risk, or cost, and will generally provoke a degree of fear and discomfort. This discomfort creates within us an urgency to address the issue. We want to solve it now, and we want to be certain of the solution. We tend to "shift the burden" of dealing with the underlying problem to short-term quick fixes, which at the time seem intuitive, appear to be effective, and temporarily relieve our discomfort. The trouble is, we never really address the underlying problem, and the situation only gets worse.

Business people have a comfort zone when it comes to money. This comfort zone is established principally by two factors. The first is their budget approval authority. The second is their tolerance for spending, which is established by experience and organizational norms. They hold strong beliefs regarding what constitutes "a lot of money." For one person, a lot of money might be $20,000, for another, it might be $2,000,000. People will usually not undertake projects that fall beyond these thresholds. Further, their belief regarding what is "a lot of money" also skews their perception of what you should be able to accomplish with "that kind of money." From the outset, without any real concept of the scale and complexity of the effort at hand, they will form expectations for timelines and budgets strongly influenced by these beliefs. People are often surprised and dismayed (and sometimes angered) when the budget reality of an important project falls beyond these expectations. The perception of personal risk increases dramatically with the size of the budget figure and the degree to which it exceeds these personal thresholds. There is the risk that the project will not be approved because the budget figure is too large. There is the risk associated with being personally responsible for the success of a large project with a large sum of money on the line. In these uncomfortable situations, clients are strongly incentivized to put tremendous pressure on systems integrators and consultants during the planning and estimating process to provide unrealistic project schedules and budgets.

Sales people whose livelihoods depend on the next sale, and consulting companies that live and die by the next project, are strongly incentivized to tell the client what they want to hear. Keeping consultants billable isn't just a nice thing for consulting companies (or individual consultants for that matter). It is absolutely mandatory. It is a matter of survival. A persistent client, advocating strongly for lower estimates, can easily introduce doubt in the thought process of the consultant. Time estimates are easy targets. They are only guesses based on experience and they are subject to great uncertainty. There is often little evidence to support them. Time and again I have witnessed members of the customer's team attempt to poke holes in a consultant's estimates by making completely unsubstantiated claims that they could do a task in less time. They rarely have the information required to make such claims. Furthermore, their claims are entirely suspect, since they are under no obligation to live by their estimates. Nevertheless, these exchanges are damaging. The thought process for the consultant goes something like this: "Maybe I'm making too big a deal out of this. Maybe I'm just being pessimistic. They understand their situation better than I do. Maybe they know something that I don't." It is not uncommon that people will convince themselves, to everyone's great peril, that they really can do the work in less time for less money.

As a consultant who is often the one who has to figure out what a project is actually going to take, I have seen this pattern more times than I can count. After re-calibrating project time and cost estimates to match actual requirements, new estimates generally exceed the originals by two to four times. In every case where I have known the people involved, it was never by intent. The client and the original sales team had simply fallen prey to the typical systemic pattern of "shifting the burden" to force the situation to mitigate their immediate fears at the expense of their future success.

The impact on trust is profound. The process itself creates resentment and distrust, which is magnified and cemented by the budget woes that inevitably follow. These are the experiences that clients and consultants take into the next project and the next relationship. They try even harder to avoid the same outcome, generally by doing exactly the same things. And the spiral continues.

"IT'S JUST BUSINESS"

The third way that we undermine the client-consultant relationship is through outright bad behavior. With all of the lip service given to the notion of "win-win" over the last two decades, many people still don't know what it really means. Many people believe that their value derives from their ability to "drive a hard bargain." They pride themselves on being tough negotiators. People don't generally set out to harm the other party. That is rarely their conscious intent. But people also generally feel that it is acceptable to approach negotiations with something less than the other party's best interests in mind. They want the advantage. They want to come out a little (or a lot) ahead of the other guy. People often look for ways to create a position of power so that they can make the other guy do what they want if necessary.

And oh, the games that we play! Some consultants will intentionally underestimate work knowing that once an effort is underway and the client has sunk real money into it, their negotiating position will be much stronger. They are willing to accept the likelihood of uncomfortable conversations in the future in order to get a project started today. It takes a lot for a client to give up on a project that is underway. Once it becomes obvious that the work cannot be done within the originally estimated budget, they ask for more money or press to trim scope. Consultants will intentionally architect solutions in ways that make their clients dependent on them for future services. Or they will attempt to create, by raising the specter of intellectual property rights infringement, situations of propriety that prevent clients from seeking help elsewhere. I have seen customers take on projects to completely redevelop entire systems just to get out from under these sorts of situations and to be rid of a consultant or consulting company.

And sometimes, clients really are trying to gain leverage with their negotiation tactics. It can be difficult to discern when a client is reacting to financial fears versus when a client is simply playing an angle. Clients know that consultants need successful projects for reference, that they cannot afford project failures, and that in the short-term, they are economically reliant on their projects. Clients exploit this reality, knowing that once their consultants are sufficiently committed, they can squeeze them for more. A favorite tactic is to get consultants to commit to time lines and budgets that they cannot possibly meet, and then to treat these as fixed bids. They question every time estimate in an attempt to get the consultant to agree to less, and at the same time do their best to cast doubt on the entire process. I once had a client tell me that our budget estimates were way too high and in the *same breath* tell me that there was no way that we could get the work done in the time that we had estimated. If clients are successful at this game, their service providers will, without fail, come up short on their budgets. Clients will then press that advantage in every ugly way imaginable.

There is the scope game. During the budgeting process, clients will grudgingly trim scope, or claim that they will take on aspects of the work themselves in order to reduce the project budget. Throughout the project they do everything they can to add the scope back in. The project tasks they said they would do don't get done, and they lean on their providers to take them on or risk the entire project falling apart.

There's the first number game. Clients press relentlessly for an initial estimate at the outset of a project. They want to know, when it is not possible to know, exactly what they are in for. They say things like, "You guys have done this before, right? Come on. You must have some idea." After a few weeks of analysis, the consultant may have enough information to hold a finger in the wind, squint into the sun, and provide a rough, order of magnitude estimate. It's amazing that clients can somehow forever remember that number but never seem to remember that it was only an estimate with a very broad margin of error. I once had a client whose first question in our very first meeting was, "So, of course, I won't hold you to this, but how long is this going to take and how much is it going to cost?" Yeah, right.

Notes

1.　Schön, Donald A. *The Reflective Practitioner: How Professionals Think in Action*. New York: Basic Books, 1983. p. 69

2.　ibid. p. 44-45

3.　Senge, Peter M. *The Fifth Discipline: The Art and Practice of the Learning Organization*. Rev. and updated ed. New York: Doubleday/Currency, 2006. p. 92-112

5.
BUILDING AN
OPERATIONAL TRUST

"Outstanding teams in organizations develop...an "operational trust," where each team member remains conscious of other team members and can be counted on to act in ways that complement each other's actions."

PETER M. SENGE [1]

It isn't hard to see how the intrinsic systemic weaknesses in the typical client-consultant relationship contribute to our failures. To mitigate our fear of complexity and uncertainty, we (clients and consultants) will have convinced ourselves that our particular situation is run-of-the-mill, and fits neatly into a well established solution pattern previously defined by others. Our fear when it comes to our financial interests will cause us to bend our perception of reality to satisfy our short-term desires. We will begin with completely unrealistic expectations of timelines and costs, to our extreme peril. Add to this our time-honored standards of bad behavior and we destroy all hope of building collaborative relationships and trust, both of which are critical to successfully solving the problems that we are ostensibly tackling together. In the process, we rob ourselves of the things that could make our careers truly rewarding: opportunities to invent new things, the possibility of making a real difference, opportunities to build lasting friendships, and the satisfaction found in simply helping one another.

Trust is inversely correlated to fear. Therefore, to build trust, we must drive out fear. The greater the extent to which we are successful, the greater the trust we will create. Driving out fear has two components. The first is recognizing and facing down our own fears. The second is learning how to ease the fears of others.

FACING DOWN OUR FEARS

Facing down our fears does not mean ignoring them or pretending that we aren't afraid. Fear is a natural human condition. No one wants to admit that they are afraid, or that they are even subject to being afraid, but in reality, we all live with it to one degree or another. The more effective we become at dealing with it, the happier we will be. Recognizing and then changing how we typically respond to fear is the first step.

Client: Recalibrate Your Expectations

As clients, one of our primary fears is that that we will be duped and taken advantage of, left to twist in the wind by incompetent, dishonest con artists who hold themselves out as "consultants." This fear is reinforced by years of bad experiences. As we have seen, the ways that we typically compensate for this fear only serve to further reinforce our perceptions. The leverage against this fear begins with taking a step back and re-calibrating our expectations.

It is appropriate and smart to seek help when faced with projects or problems that are beyond our depth. Consider as an example, a visit to the doctor. We seek the advice of a doctor because he has developed an expertise through education, training, and experience that we don't possess and really need. But a wise purchaser of medical services takes responsibility for her own care and overall health. She recognizes that she brings something to the equation that the doctor cannot: her knowledge of herself, her history, and her symptoms. She listens carefully, strives to be personally informed, and applies common sense. She uses her own judgment to determine if the advice she has been given is logical. She questions, even challenges the doctor if necessary to be sure that she understands his recommendations, and that they make sense. This exchange provides opportunities for more information to be surfaced, for a deeper understanding between the doctor and the patient, which may cause the doctor to refine his recommendations, resulting in better care and ultimately a better health outcome.

The smart patient views her doctor as a partner in helping her achieve the health outcome she desires — not hired help, not an infallible deity. She respects what he brings to the partnership, but also understands that she is responsible for her part. She is not personally invested in a particular diagnosis or course of treatment when she seeks help. She fully expects that the doctor isn't either. She understands that there are limits to the doctor's range of expertise and experience, and she fully expects that he will engage the help of other experts whom he knows and trusts. What she really wants is someone who can help her solve her problem.

To be sure, a good consultant can help you deal with the complexity of your particular situation and successfully guide you through the problem solving and solution implementation process. That is what you really need. What you don't need, and really don't want, is someone to come in and try to do what they did for some other company (probably your competitor). You don't want them to ignore or try to eliminate your uniqueness simply because they have some preconception regarding "best practices" or some generic template for how companies in your industry should work. You don't want them to try to force-fit your problem into the limited domain of their experience and expertise. You don't want them to arbitrarily force your problem to fit a particular tool set or technology simply because they are professionally invested in it.

With this set of expectations, it is much easier to evaluate the people before you. You are clear regarding your responsibilities in the process. You know what to look for, and in particular, the things that should raise the red flags for you. You can clearly communicate your expectations.

Client: Embrace Your Uniqueness

Another fear that drives our behavior as clients is our fear of complexity, and all that comes with it. As we have seen, a common response to this fear is to attempt to explain it away, or to otherwise pretend that it doesn't exist. One way that organizations commonly do this is by convincing themselves that they really are not unique in any meaningful way, and that any real uniqueness is probably a bad thing, arising from operational anomalies or poor practices. The leverage against this fear is straightforward, but counter intuitive — recognize and embrace the uniqueness of your organization. Uniqueness is not a problem to be managed. Sustainable competitive advantage in any industry is achieved by creating a unique and valuable position that your competitors cannot easily duplicate.[2] It is about being intentionally different from your competitors, in a way that delivers a unique type of value to your customers. We see two common mistakes that company's make. The first is obsessing over best practices. Research into and an examination of best practices is appropriate at the outset of a transformational effort as an educational undertaking and to provide a framework to build upon. But always remember that best practices were not developed with your company in mind. "Sameness" for the sake of sameness has no value. Furthermore, "commonly followed" by no means ensures "best". The false benchmark of best practices will often lead people to discard truly innovative new ideas and techniques, simply because they are not widely accepted. Besides, who is to say that your company's practices aren't actually better, especially when you consider the uniqueness of your market position?

The second mistake that we commonly see is when companies convince themselves that they are operationally something that they are not. Here is an example. I once worked on a project for a travel company who needed to make significant changes to their systems in order to stay competitive in their industry against the likes of Orbitz and Expedia. As a travel company, they did what travel companies do: offer vacation packages, help customers create vacation plans, book reservations, and so on. But at some point in the company's history, they had convinced themselves (or were convinced by someone) that operationally, they were really just a manufacturer. They "manufactured" vacations for customers from an "inventory" of available options. Then, at what was surely a significant cost with significant effort, they implemented SAP ERP as their primary operational system.

If you close one eye, squint the other, and hit yourself hard in the head with a hammer a few times, you might kind of see how a travel agency is like a manufacturer. Like a round peg in a square hole, it's simply awkward. In an attempt to make life simpler, they only made it harder. As a result, when the time came that they desperately needed to evolve their systems in order to survive, the problem was extremely complex. As we worked to understand the nature of the problem at hand and what we needed to do to solve it, we were burdened by a persistent intellectual overhead that resulted from having to constantly translate the domain of travel into the domain of manufacturing. This overhead held absolutely no value to the business, and served only to burn intellectual cycles that could have been put to much better use. They would have been so much better off had they simply accepted that as a travel company, their domain is what it is, with its own unique qualities, complexities and challenges rather than try to force-fit their operations into an inappropriate model.

Consultant: Recognize the Source of Your Value

For consultants, one of our primary fears is that someone might find out that we don't really have all the answers. But real effectiveness is not derived from knowing every answer to any question that may present itself. Real effectiveness derives from being able to figure out the answers along the way. By assuming that you must know everything, you limit yourself to only tackling problems that you know. That sounds somewhat reasonable until you realize that you never see the same situation twice. Therefore, if you rely only on your narrow set of technical skills and experiences, you are actually quite limited in the situations in which you will be truly effective.

Your background, comprised of your education, experience, and skills, is very valuable. But your value is not in the list of projects that you have worked on, the tools that you have mastered, or the degrees and certifications that you may have amassed. It is in your increased capacity to *do*. This capacity determines your ability to cut through the noise and identify what is truly important, to grasp complexity and explain it in a way that everyone can understand, and to invent new and appropriate solutions. It grows with your emotional maturity and your ability to deal effectively with people. It grows with your education and experience. It has no limits, and no expiration. As long as you continue to learn and to improve, your capacity will continue to grow.

Conversely, if you define your value in terms of the particular set of tools that you have mastered, then you have limited your capacity to problems appropriate to that toolset. Whether that is some set of best practices, patterns, or software products, your tendency will be to apply your toolset formulaically. Your capacity will grow only as much as your knowledge of your toolset grows. In the field of IT, you are constantly at risk of obsolescence, and will periodically find yourself at the bottom of the heap as you struggle to re-tool.

To a certain degree, it's a matter of being comfortable in your own skin. It's not overconfidence or arrogance, but self-assurance in your ability to help the client and add value. It's being willing to stretch professionally to meet the challenges of a given situation, but also the wisdom to recognize your limits. It is a balance that shows up as professional poise. Young or old, if you can master this, it will take you far.

Embrace Being Wrong

As consultants, we also deeply fear being wrong. Those of us who work in the field of IT as programmers, architects, business analysts, and project managers are highly analytical by nature. A common characteristic of analytical types, which also includes mathematicians, engineers, and scientists, is that we *hate to be wrong*. We react viscerally to the prospect of being wrong. The reaction can be very strong, invoking fear and anger, not unlike a fight-or-flight response. It is very uncomfortable for us, and to avoid this discomfort, *we need to be right*. Compound this with the fact that we tend to be very competitive with significant egos, and consultants can be downright insufferable.

Paradoxically, being willing to be wrong means that you will get to right faster. It is not uncommon that an initial impression, recommendation, or plan of action turns out to be wrong. It's the nature of the work. We form opinions and choose directions based on the information at hand, which is always incomplete. As new information becomes available, and we learn more, we may form new opinions and choose different directions. This is perfectly acceptable and is actually a sign of a healthy, well functioning process. Problem solving is an iterative process of learning, in which being wrong is not only likely, but often necessary. Defending a position out of fear of being wrong only wastes time and delays the process of getting to right.

MONETARY POLICY

Our fear responses to financial issues are real and they are powerful. There is no leverage in ignoring them or in pretending that we are not subject to their influence. If we acknowledge them and tackle them head-on, there are some simple things that we can do to mitigate their influence.

Set the boundaries

The first thing we have to do is to set the boundaries for the conversations. The idea is to agree to some basic parameters of schedule and cost before diving into the details. One thing that we all want to avoid is sinking a bunch of time into this process only to find out at the end that we are miles apart on schedule and budget. The more time we invest, the more likely we are to succumb to the influence of our fears. Think of it as passing through a series of gates, and you can't proceed to the next gate until you have successfully passed through the one you are currently facing.

Agree to Rates

The first gate is to agree to rates. There is no reason to continue if you can't get through this gate. There will likely be an issue if a client is used to paying $50 per hour and the consulting company's rates are $150 per hour. If the consulting company has a value proposition that is compelling to the client, and can make the case for its rates, then an agreement will be reached. If not, then there is no sense in wasting everyone's time. This issue becomes much more emotional and harder to deal with when it is clouded by other factors, such as time estimates, and after everyone has invested a bunch of time in the process. Time is money for all parties. If you are not going to be able to agree on rates, better to know that in the first hour rather than three weeks into the process.

Understand Scope

It is critical that everyone has a common understanding of roughly what must be done to achieve the stated objectives of the effort. It is neither realistic nor required at this point that we have a complete statement of requirements, but we must have an explicit, mutual understanding of the business problem to be solved (problem statement) and what the target solution might be (system vision).

This may seem obvious, but it is not uncommon that clients and their consultants hold vastly different ideas and opinions regarding what needs to be done, and start talking about timelines and costs without ever really clarifying that they are talking about the same thing; I'm talking about a 100,000 square foot warehouse space, your talking about a 100,000 square foot office building. These are easy conversations to have early in the process, where the client educates the consultant as to the nature of the business problem or opportunity, and the consultant educates the client regarding potential solutions. The conversations are much more difficult and emotional once we are trying to reconcile proposed costs with expectations.

Understand Budget Limits

This is a tough one for clients. There is the fear that estimates will magically grow to meet a stated budget. This fear is not unfounded, but as a client, it doesn't serve you to keep this information to yourself. There are other ways to mitigate this risk. For example, if you have made it to this gate, you have already agreed to rates with your service provider and you have a mutual understanding of scope. This limits the factors available to the service provider to manipulate should it be tempted to inflate its estimates to match the available budget.

If you have a $100,000 budget and a $1,000,000 problem, it is better to know sooner rather than later. An experienced consultant can tell you fairly quickly and with a reasonable degree of certainty if your budget is at least within a stone's throw of your objectives. This does not mean that you have to know exactly what the budget is, or that the consultant must know the exact cost. This is not a commitment by either party, simply a decision to proceed or not. You may decide to proceed by digging deeper on time estimates. You may decide to re-evaluate your anticipated scope relative to your business objectives. If there is no way to accomplish something meaningful from a business perspective within the available budget, it is in no one's interest to continue. This is in no way a failure. It's smart business.

Understand Time Limits

Finally, if there are real time constraints, it is important to get them in the open as soon as possible. By real, I mean time constraints resulting from real business conditions: competitive response, contractual obligations, and so on. Better to address time constraints early on to determine whether or not they can be feasibly met. As with the budget conversations, it is not necessary that you and your consultant agree to exactly how long something is going to take. You are only trying to detect vast discrepancies between needs (or expectations) and reality. If you need something in three months that could take a year to implement, either some adjustments will need to be made or there is no point in continuing.

Separation of Concerns: Effort vs. Cost

Whether you are talking about an entire project or a small change request, always understand and agree on a reasonable estimate of effort before talking about how much it will cost. What is a reasonable estimate? One that is explainable, defendable, and *reasoned*. Preferably, it is one that you and your service provider work out *together*. We do this because cost will skew our perception of effort nearly every time. If everyone can look at an estimate of effort, understand it, and agree to it, then the cost estimate is simple multiplication. You may not be thrilled with the result, but you will have removed any doubt regarding how you got there.

Once you have solid estimates of effort and cost, you can now reasonably assess them against budget and time limits. Again, you won't necessarily be happy with the answer, but you will at least have the facts. If everyone is willing to face those facts, subsequent conversations will be less emotional and more productive. Rather than arguing over the numbers, we can put our heads together to figure out if there are ways to bring them in line with our constraints.

Win-Win or No Deal[3]-- Seriously

Win-win is straight-forward in concept but difficult in practice. We fear that we will have to sacrifice what matters most to us, because we think win-win is really about compromise, and compromise is really about lose-lose. We fear that if we enter into negotiations with genuine intentions, but the other party doesn't, then we will be in a position of weakness and will be taken advantage of (lose-win). But if you were able to set the boundaries of rates, scope, budget, and time, and you were able to separate the concerns of effort vs. cost, then you are most of the way there. The facts are on the table. There is nothing hidden that can be manipulated. Everyone's needs are clear: for the client, budget and time; for the consultant, effort and rates. Scope is clear and explicit. There is no point in trying to manipulate these factors in an attempt to "drive a hard bargain" since any effort to do so would be obvious, and would be seen as disingenuous.

There will certainly be times when we will not be able to come to terms, and that is perfectly fine. A consultant may not be able to do the work at the rates that are economically feasible for the client. The client may not have the money to invest. In these situations, the right thing to do is to shake hands and say, "Thanks, maybe next time." And if you played by these rules, there will likely be a next time, because there will be no hard feelings, and you will have built a strong relationship of trust.

EASING THE FEARS OF OTHERS

The Willingness to Be Vulnerable

In his book, *Getting Naked*, Patrick Lencioni wrote, "Without the willingness to be vulnerable, we will not build deep and lasting relationships in life. That's because there is no better way to earn a person's trust than by putting ourselves in a position of unprotected weakness and demonstrating that we believe they will support us." He goes on to explain how prevailing social mores that require us "to always project strength, confidence, and poise" ultimately "stifle our ability to build trust."[4]

In our field (and perhaps in the entire business world) excessive competitiveness is the rule. We are all so concerned with being perceived and acknowledged as the "best" and the "brightest" that our principal concern becomes building and protecting our own image and never "looking bad." Whenever you or someone else bases an argument for or against something on "not looking bad," that argument will be invalid nearly every time. In fact, it's a good sign that you are actually on the right track. In other words, if it makes you uncomfortable, it's probably the right thing to do.

Be quick to point out your mistakes and your errors in your thinking. Never be afraid to ask the "stupid" questions. Probably eight out of ten times, someone else in the room has the same question and is just afraid to ask. Never hesitate to say, "I don't know, but I can find out." Laugh at your own expense. Humor puts people at ease. It lets people know that you don't take yourself too seriously. You will find that if you are willing to do these things, people will cut you a lot of slack, because they know that you will do the same for them.

Treat People as Trustworthy

Peter Senge noted that often, the only way to break an escalating cycle of distrust is through an overt act of trust.[5] One such overt act is to treat people as essentially trustworthy. Here is a question: How do you respond when other people automatically assume that you are untrustworthy? Do you find yourself deeply motivated to earn their trust and to prove them wrong? Do you feel that they, in return, must be trustworthy? Probably not. Our natural response is protective. Our first conclusion, which is likely correct, is that in the event of trouble we can't rely on the other person to meet us half-way to resolve a problem. We are immediately on guard and suspicious. We now view the other party as untrustworthy, which reinforces their assumptions of us, and off we go. It can be very difficult to break this cycle once it has begun.

It is important that we treat people as worthy of our trust until proven otherwise. There are a couple of realizations that can help us do this. First is the realization that our self-interests are largely bound to the self-interests of the other party. It is really as simple as this: if they don't succeed, you will not succeed, and vice versa. There really is no middle ground here. Any other position is predicated on failure, and who will come out better in the event of failure. The reality is, if we fail, no one will come out well. That is a simple, brutal fact. It does not matter how well you protect yourself, there is no scenario where things can turn out badly for the other guy and at the same time turn out well for you.

The second is realizing that taking the stance that other people are inherently untrustworthy does us no good anyway. It doesn't cause people to be trustworthy, and it does nothing to improve our outcomes. Trust cannot be enforced. It cannot be demanded. It is demonstrated and earned. By treating people as trustworthy, you set them at ease. You take the first step toward earning their trust and you give them the opportunity to earn yours.

Does this mean we take a Pollyanna view that there aren't any bad actors in the world? Of course not. Does it mean we will never be disappointed? No. That's why we have contracts. They set forth the terms of engagement in detail so that everyone knows their responsibilities, how things will work (time tracking, remittance of payment, expense reporting, and so forth), what conditions constitute a fundamental breach, and how conflicts will be resolved if necessary. Good contracts put everyone at ease.

Seeing Each Other as Colleagues

People naturally feel vulnerable expressing their ideas freely in front of their superiors, or in front of someone they feel is vastly more qualified than they are, often with good reason. This vulnerability is reinforced when people of rank feel threatened and indignant when a "subordinate" speaks out of school, or challenges them. Even after many years of experience, I am personally subject to this feeling of vulnerability. Not long ago, I found myself in a conference room full of people and a client executive who simply refused to set aside her position of rank and authority. She made it absolutely clear that there were topics that were off-limits and above my pay grade. This left me fighting back my own sense of exposure, while trying to dance around sensitive issues that needed to be addressed. It made everyone uncomfortable, and unfortunately, nothing of substance was accomplished until after she left the room.

On highly-functioning teams, team members treat each other as equals and colleagues regardless of position. They absolutely believe that on their own, they would each fail, and they truly value what the other team members bring to the equation. This is critical because it creates the safety that people need to speak openly. Moreover, Senge points out that people who see each other as friends and colleagues interact differently. "We talk differently with friends from the way we do with people who are not friends."[6] When we can achieve this level of interaction, great things happen, and it starts with simply seeing each other as equals.

It takes practice to learn to recognize the patterns of behavior that sabotage our relationships and torpedo our efforts. It's a little like learning to recognize a recurring dream while you are having it. These patterns are so pervasive and so automatic that we have to be consciously on the look out for them and learn to control our own responses appropriately. Furthermore, the techniques for facing down our fears and easing the fears of others are simple and intuitive in principle, but remarkably difficult to adopt.

One reason that it is difficult is that there really are bad actors out there, though not nearly as many as you may think. There are two kinds: those who have consciously bad intentions to begin with, and those whose character will crumble under pressure. These are the people who will disappoint you and make you question the wisdom of trust. But that's why it's called a *discipline*. You have to have the courage and tenacity to stick with it, even when things go wrong.

The good news is that the more you stick with it, the easier it becomes to recognize the bad actors sooner. You will find that these people will resist your attempts to build trust. They will take advantage of your vulnerability. They will resist collegiality. Despite your best efforts, they will fall back to the standard patterns of behavior. The ability to spot these people sooner allows you to be more selective in your choices of service providers and clients. And being selective is critical. There is no point in going down the path with someone whom you cannot trust. You simply won't succeed.

This is particularly difficult for service providers. You must be willing to walk away from a project. This is where your power lies. If you aren't willing to to say, "thanks, but no thanks," then this is all just talk. You will have no real ability to improve your outcomes.

Again, this is why it's a discipline. You will have to walk away at some point. Choosing what projects not to do is just as important, if not more so, than choosing the projects to undertake.

The payoffs are real, and far from trivial. As a consultant, you will build deep and long-lasting relationships with clients. Year after year they will seek you out to ask for help with the next effort, big or small. You will enjoy a more consistent book of business. You will spend less time selling and the time that you do spend will be more focused and fruitful. You will spend less time reading contracts, less time dealing with troubled projects, less time extracting yourself from bad situations, less time protecting yourself, and less time talking to lawyers.

You will do more work that you truly enjoy. And as you work with clients over the long term, you will get to see the fruits of your efforts pay off in their successes. You will actually make a difference, rather than simply running on the mouse wheel. You will spend more time solving business problems, creating, and innovating. Not only is this far more enjoyable, it is also wildly more productive. And make no mistake: higher productivity translates to cold, hard, cash.

As a client, you will spend less time trying to find good help, writing requests for service, reading resumes, and interviewing consultants. You will spend less time clubbing consultants over the head, protecting yourself, and trying to eject bad consultants off of your projects. The constantly revolving door of mediocre consultants will slow as you build relationships with people you can trust, and who really can help. With it will go the cost of starting over again and again with new consultants who have to ramp up in your environment and learn your business before they can become truly productive (if they ever do). You will experience fewer false starts on projects, fewer failures, and much better results overall. The cost savings alone will be enormous, but the benefit to the business will be far greater than just the money saved. More of your effort will be spent productively improving the business and building better solutions faster.

Notes

1. Senge, Peter M. *The Fifth Discipline: The Art and Practice of the Learning Organization.* Rev. and updated. ed. New York: Doubleday/Currency, 2006. p. 219

2. Porter, Michael E. "Strategy and the Internet." *Harvard Business Review OnPoint,* (2001).

3. Covey, Stephen R. *The 7 Habits of Highly Successful People.* 25th Anniversary Edition. RosettaBooks LLC, 2013. p. 215-245

4. Lencioni, Patrick. *Getting Naked: A Business Fable About Shedding the Three Fears That Sabotage Client Loyalty.* San Francisco, CA: Jossey-Bass, 2010. p.vii

5. ibid. 1, p. 395
    Senge describes in the management principle of the Escalation pattern that cycles of aggression can be reversed by taking overtly aggressive "peaceful" actions. I extrapolated that idea to reversing escalating cycles of distrust with "overt acts of trust."

6. ibid. 1, p. 265
    It is interesting to note that Drucker, in Post-Capitalist Society (page 128), hits on the idea of collegiality as well, but explains it in the context of knowledge-based work and knowledge-based organizations: "Because modern organization is an organization of knowledge specialists it has to be an organization of equals, of 'colleagues' of 'associates'. No knowledge 'ranks' higher than another. The position of each is determined by its contribution to the common task rather than by any inherent superiority or inferiority 'Philosophy is the Queen of the Sciences' says an old tag. But to remove a kidney stone you want a urologist rather than a logician. The modern organization cannot be an organization of 'boss' and 'subordinate'. It must be organized as a team of 'associates'."

PART 2:
THE DISCIPLINE OF CLARITY

It is another paradox of the human condition that we have virtually unlimited ability to create complexity, but limited ability (or more accurately, willingness) to understand it and deal with it. We are enormously inventive. We create wonderful, intricate things, many of them wildly complex. In business and industry, advances in technology have eliminated — or at least vastly reduced — natural limits on scale and scope. Communication and information technology in particular has enabled unprecedented flexibility in building, and then changing, our value chains. It has enabled the creation of entirely new products and services that were previously unimaginable, and has enabled us to sell and deliver them on a scale that is difficult to grasp. We have enabled ourselves to create enterprises and industries of a complexity that is beyond our ability to understand. It is possible for us to create business enterprises that behave like ecological systems, where without deep understanding of the system itself, any given action is likely to result in unanticipated and undesirable consequences. The problem is, we can easily build houses of cards and not really recognize it. We march happily along assuming a degree of rationality, robustness, and durability that simply doesn't exist. We are rolling coal trains over bridges of cardboard, and too often, we are completely surprised when they collapse.

Understandably, complexity makes us uneasy. Complexity introduces the possibility that we won't be able to solve the problem at hand — that when we pull back the covers and really look, we will find that we have dramatically underestimated its scope and scale. We will not be able to solve the problem in time for it to matter, in the time that we have arbitrarily assigned, or within the budget that we have arbitrarily set. Complexity means uncertainty, and uncertainty means risk. Risk means that we may fail, lose our jobs, and ruin our careers. We may no longer be able to provide for our families. This is fundamental, visceral, life and death variety fear. Watch carefully, and you will see the ways it drives us all.

When faced with complexity, we are tempted to oversimplify it or explain it away. We tend to try to side-step it by seeking out sameness, patterns of understanding, formulae, or best practices. But the fact is that we are better served when we face it head-on. We are actually quite capable of understanding complexity. It is not a matter of over-simplification or denial, but rather a willingness and the discipline to acknowledge and embrace it; to expand our capacity to grasp it and to hold it before us in a useful way in order to achieve *clarity*.

Clarity is our weapon against complexity, which tends to dissolve before us as we become clear. It's not that the complexity isn't real, it's that we increase our capacity to *understand*. Clarity in some respects is an outcome of learning. But it is a special outcome. It is the acquisition of knowledge, and something more: Discovery, synthesis, understanding, *lucidity*. Clarity is about the "aha" moments, the emergence of entirely new ideas. For transformational efforts, clarity is not optional. It is the minimum requirement for creativity and innovation.

A *discipline* of clarity is the body of theory and technique that must be studied, mastered, and put into practice to achieve clarity in a repeatable, predictable, and productive way. A discipline of clarity requires two commitments. The first is a commitment to the acquisition of a shared understanding. The acquisition of shared understanding requires rigorously and systematically surfacing, expressing, and exercising our internal pictures of how things work. The goal is to develop explicit, formalized, shared models versus implicit informal mental (internal) models. By explicit, formalized, and shared, I mean out there for all to see, expressed in a standardized and formal manner (sorry, no scribbled-on cocktail napkins). Knowledge is fleeting, so care must be taken to adequately capture and preserve it. That which goes unstated, remains unknown. By models, I literally mean expressing a logical simulation of the solution-to-be, and then mentally exercising it, or *practicing* [1] with it, in order to sufficiently define, understand, and refine *what* the solution needs to be.

The second is a commitment to being honest with ourselves, both individually and as a team. It is impossible to see clearly from behind the blindfold of self-deception. This is different from, but a prerequisite to, being honest with each other. It is a characteristic of leadership that Jim Collins calls "confronting the brutal facts,"[2] and what Peter Senge calls a "commitment to the truth."[3] It is a commitment to being clear regarding the current reality: where you stand now versus where you want to be. This includes being willing to ask, and able to answer the hard questions regarding schedule and budget; being able to admit when we are stuck and need help; being able to admit when we don't know; being able to admit when we need more time; being able to admit when we underestimated a task, and so on. This requires that we have in place the mechanisms and the protocols required to recognize, acknowledge, and deal with problems as early as possible.

More importantly, it requires a unified commitment to a successful outcome above all else: above our need to never be wrong, to never admit mistakes, to never be the one to blame. This frees us from fear and allows us to face and solve problems together as a team, rather than waste time on the typical activities of avoidance, finger pointing, and denial. This is where the discipline of trust and the discipline of clarity intersect. It is to some degree an act of courage to face the facts of the situation, particularly when the facts are not good. This is when the principles of driving out fear matter the most, and pay the highest dividends. Adversity happens. It cannot be overcome if you are not first willing to acknowledge it.

Notes

1.   Schön, Donald A. *The Reflective Practitioner: How Professionals Think in Action.*
      New York: Basic Books, 1983. p. 157-162

      Schön describes the concept of "virtual worlds" that practitioners construct to
      essentially simulate the "real world of practice." In his example, he describes
      how two architects working together use quick drawings and sketches to
      model and test their ideas:

      "In his virtual world, the practitioner can manage some of the constraints to
      hypothesis-testing experiment which are inherent to the world of his practice.
      Hence his ability to construct and manipulate virtual worlds is a crucial
      component of his ability to not only perform artistically, but to experiment
      rigorously."

      He goes on to describe how, while "the act of drawing can be rapid and
      spontaneous," the ideas remain stable and can be examined at leisure. The
      designer can go fast or slow down to think, and ideas that would take a
      long time to realize in the real world can happen immediately in the virtual
      world. This is a profound insight that describes the true power of modeling:
      to facilitate creativity while at the same time providing the practitioner the
      means to "experiment rigorously," or in other words to simulate an idea prior
      to realizing it.

2.   Collins, Jim. *Good to Great: Why Some Companies Make the Leap...And Others
      Don't*: HarperBusiness, 2011. iBooks. https://itun.es/us/yhVOA.l. p. 129-165

3.   Senge, Peter M. *The Fifth Discipline: The Art and Practice of the Learning
      Organization.* Rev. and updated ed. New York: Doubleday/Currency, 2006. p.
      148-151.

6.
ACQUIRING A SHARED
UNDERSTANDING

The first requirement for clarity is the acquisition of a shared understanding. It goes without saying that it is very difficult to solve a problem that you do not fully understand. Further, it is awfully hard to create a solution when you aren't clear regarding what needs to be done. An individual or a small team working on a small problem can slug their way through it, iterating over the problem until they get it right. It may be inefficient, but it is at least possible. For a large team, this is practically impossible, because to effectively iterate over the problem, they must at least share a common understanding of what they are ultimately trying to accomplish so that they can iterate collectively. As obvious as this seems, the acquisition of shared understanding is the most often neglected aspect of transformational efforts. There are many reasons why: it is difficult, time-consuming, and largely intangible in terms of what people typically associate with value (such as software). It is hard for people to perceive in the moment how clarity, or the lack of it, will affect their final outcome. The required skill set is difficult to cultivate. The traditional "not-so-best-practices" and current "best" practices that we employ are neither effective for capturing the understanding that we acquire, nor effective for facilitating the process of acquisition.

One such practice is to rely on tribal knowledge and word-of-mouth. In snippets of conversation between two or three people, bits of information are exchanged, and decisions are made. Some of this information might make it into a document somewhere, but most of it doesn't. Individuals proceed with their tasks, auspiciously as a team, but with vastly different understandings of the problem and the solution vision. These differences are rarely surfaced until much further down the road when problems arise.

This approach certainly seems expedient, particularly at the beginning of a project when project teams are small and the amount of information is manageable. Given the inevitable time and budget pressure, it is always tempting to abandon a more rigorous approach for the sake of "getting things done." Inevitably, the amount of information that people have to carry around in their heads becomes overwhelming. Details, and even entire discussions are forgotten. The shared understanding achieved in the quick conversation lasts as long as the conversation itself.

At the other end of the spectrum, a practice that continues to persist is the traditional waterfall approach and the bulleted list of "shall" statements. Despite what might seem to be a universal understanding of its deficiencies, I am frequently greeted on new projects with the dreaded "requirements document." I have been presented with lists of literally thousands of "shall" statements and told that all I have to do is to read them and I will know everything that the system is supposed to do. But in reality this is like taking delivery of a new car by having a dump truck back up and dump a pile of car parts in front of you while the car salesman hands you the keys. The car is certainly not very useful in that form, and there is really no way of knowing, by simply looking at the pile, if all the parts are really there, or if the car will work when you put them together. You can't even be sure that you're getting the right car. These documents, created at immense cost and tremendous pain and suffering also come with the personal investment of their authors, who generally don't take kindly to the suggestion that more needs to be done.

The backlash to this approach has been the rise of Agile methods. The antithesis of the waterfall approach, Agile eschews almost all forms of requirements documentation, seeing it as redundant to the software itself. There are many aspects of Agile methods that are truly excellent and useful, but the clarity of requirements is not one of them. In many ways, Agile amounts to giving up on solving the problem of clarity altogether. The idea is that the only way we will really ever understand what the system is supposed to do is to build it. If we break it up and build it in really small bits, in the end all of those small bits will magically manifest into the cohesive, well thought out and complete system that we have imagined. This approach is analogous to a team of people sitting around the pile of car parts picking out things they like and trying to piece them together. One guy likes a wheel, so he starts with that. Another guy decides to start with a piston. What is the likelihood that they ever actually succeed in putting the car together, much less on time and within budget?

And finally, we are incredibly bad at engaging teams of people in the creative process and conducting productive conversation. People very rarely invest the time and effort required to develop a complete and accurate common understanding of what they are trying to accomplish and what they need to do. It is not so much that people are afraid to do this, or that they don't want to. They just don't know how and don't have the means for doing it. The task often seems overwhelming, and it requires tremendous discipline to successfully complete. Getting started is very difficult, like trying to eat an elephant with a spoon. People come together, often for the first time, in cramped, uncomfortable conference rooms. Generally, everyone has some perception of the problem domain. But without exception, our understanding, individually and collectively will be incomplete, over-simplified, and in many ways inaccurate. Without some formal means of surfacing this reality, even figuring out where to begin can be an enormous challenge. And the clock is ticking.

With no real way to effectively begin to unravel the complexity of the problem domain, the situation quickly degrades. In their earnestness to make progress, people begin the brain dump process. With many people in a room, this is characterized by a great deal of disorganized conversation, where much is said, but very little is revealed. People are anxious to share what they consider to be the most important, complex (and minute) details that they know. These are generally the things that worry them, that they are afraid will be missed if they don't mention them right away. People talk past each other, over each other, and in circles. What one person feels is critical, another thinks is trivial, and arguments begin to ensue. Business analysts and project managers furiously take notes, trying (in vain) to capture the snippets of what seem like important details that fly by. Subject matter experts become frustrated and overwhelmed, not only because no one seems to be "getting it," but mostly because they are struggling deeply to properly express their thoughts and concerns. Project managers become frustrated and overwhelmed because of the lack of progress with no end in sight. Business analysts are frustrated and overwhelmed because they feel as if they are trying to drink from a fire hose, and they have a growing sense that they aren't keeping up.

Frustration and being overwhelmed trigger fear which in turn triggers people's defensive mechanisms. Within a few days or maybe a week, the situation begins to degrade. Conversations are characterized by loud debate, where people take positions and strongly defend them, often over trivial details. Feelings get hurt. Fewer people actually participate in the process, generally only talking when the conversation is directed at them. Conversations become dominated by a few people, usually those with some position of authority and strong opinions. As the clock continues to tick, there is enormous pressure to produce a requirements definition. Under this pressure, combined with the discomfort and pure tedium of the process, the team will convince itself that an understanding has been reached, and that the requirements definition is "good enough." Secretly, people will harbor grave reservations, but it is almost guaranteed that no one will express them. And of course, how could they? Without the means to adequately express the requirements to begin with, how could they possibly express how they are wrong or incomplete?

Despite their emphasis on communication, Agile methods are only slightly better. This is not because the concepts are wrong, but rather because there is generally no common frame of reference to provide structure and meaning to the conversation. We will "burn it down" every day. We will stand so that we will keep it short and only talk about stuff that really matters. I'll talk about my progress and problems trying to attach the wheels to the car. You'll talk about trying to attach the piston to the crank-shafty-thing — lot's of small, shallow conversation about details that seem important at the moment, but lack the context of shared understanding.

Every few weeks, we select a group of user stories from the backlog to implement. This is analogous to sifting through the pile of car parts to decide what we should pull out and try to assemble next. The trick is, that by design, the pile of parts is never complete. We are continually adding parts to the pile (or taking them away) as we discover things we think we need (or don't). Every few weeks when we get together to sift through the backlog, we're dealing with a different set of parts. Without the guiding light of a broader vision and shared understanding, the design of the car takes a random walk. It's like trying to reach a specific destination in unfamiliar territory while driving in dense fog and never bothering to look at a map. Eventually, we end up somewhere, but probably not where we wanted. What is truly maddening is that the fog is of our own making, and we *choose* to not look at the map.

Clearly, there must be a better way, and of course there is. But how will we recognize it? How can we be sure that what we choose will be better than what we have already tried and that it won't just be more of the same — doing too little, or doing too much, and in the end still not achieving the real clarity that we are seeking? As with solving any problem, the answer lies in first understanding *what* you are trying to accomplish.

THE REQUIREMENTS DEFINITION

The most critical and tangible artifact that contributes to the acquisition of a shared understanding is the requirements definition. As a set of deliverables, this definition should provide the stakeholders with a reference that persists over time. It should guide ongoing efforts, remind team members about what was decided, what needs to be done, and what they are trying to accomplish. It is a mechanism for communicating clearly to the broader business community and for bringing new project members up to speed quickly.

But the bigger purpose of the requirements definition – the acquisition of a shared understanding – is realized in the process of its creation. Shared understanding is captured by the deliverables, but it is achieved in the process of expressing and capturing ideas, through productive conversation, and through creation and invention. It is during this process that we define the nature of our envisioned reality. This is the vision we are investing in, which will largely define the success of our clients (or employers) for years to come. Its importance cannot be over-emphasized. Millions of dollars are on the line and it is the quality of this effort that to a great extent will determine if that money is wisely invested or wasted.

We define requirements in order to describe what a system must do in order to improve the business in a material way. This is, after all, the reason why companies invest in technology to begin with.

This is arguably when the most important work happens. The goal is to invent a solution to capitalize on an opportunity or to solve a problem. To do this effectively requires bringing together a diverse group of people from across many disciplines and leveraging their experiences, knowledge, and intellects. Some very heavy lifting occurs in this process. This is the time when smart and impassioned people have the chance to really make a difference by creating new and great things.

In order to successfully acquire a share understanding, the process of defining requirements and the outcome of this process, the requirements definition, must meet certain requirements of their own.

The activity of defining requirements shall facilitate creation and invention

In order for the activity of defining requirements to be meaningful, it must actually advance us toward our goals. Too often, the analysis effort, which we know is important to our ultimate success, becomes a source of frustration and delay. As we move through the process, a sense of futility grows. We begin to feel that there are more questions than answers. We try get our arms around the information and the complexity, but to no avail. At some point in the process, we find that we are only treading water, waiting for the real work to begin.

A good analysis process is principally focused on facilitating creation and invention. The documentation of that creation and invention, the requirements definition itself, is only a by-product. A good process will be self-documenting, and the act of documenting will actually facilitate the process. You will know you have it right when you begin to feel that this activity is absolutely essential, not just a milestone to get through.

A requirements definition shall be free of mechanism

The requirements for the system must specify what the system must do to meet the stated objectives of the business. The requirements definition is not a "high-level design." When done well, it is a purely logical model of the system to be. Any mention of mechanisms, such as databases, programming languages, packaged software applications, or the like, is strictly off limits for two very good reasons.

First, if we start thinking about how we will do something during the process of defining what to do, we are highly susceptible to arbitrarily limiting the requirements based on what we currently know how to do, or what we think we can do. This is the typical pattern that underlies our tendency to cut the practice situation to fit within the current limits of our knowledge and skill. This also puts a serious throttle on creativity and innovation. How can we invent anything new if we limit our thought process only to what we currently believe we can do?

Second, for the vast majority of us, our brains are not good at trying to answer two questions at once. The mental exercise of trying to figure out the complex interdependencies between what and how is challenging even after we are clear on what we need to do. As a running exercise while we are otherwise occupied with the challenging task of inventing what the solution is, and while that definition is constantly changing, it is overwhelming. It is simply beyond the ability of most of us. Fortunately, it is quite possible, and in fact very effective, to answer these questions in sequence. It does, however, require a high degree of mental discipline as well as practice to keep these concerns separate.

A requirements definition shall tell a story

The requirements definition must provide adequate context for understanding. Context includes intent: Why are we doing this and how will the business be improved in a material way? Intent acts as a lighthouse to keep us off the rocks. It guides our actions and decisions. It helps us to understand and remember what is important and what is not. It helps us define our desired outcomes. But beyond intent, context allows us to visualize the whole. It's not until we can all begin to see how the whole fits together that the solution can truly be visualized. You will know you have it right when the solution begins to jump out at you and becomes obvious. And not just to you, but to the team as a whole. When you reach this point, people will literally not be able to suppress talking about *how*, and the conversation will naturally progress from requirements to design.

A requirements definition shall be self-contained

The requirements definition should not require a team of experts to explain. It does not require supporting documentation to be understandable. It is complete in and of itself. If it isn't in the requirements definition, it doesn't exist. In the beginning, people will refer to many sources of requirements, including other documents, subject matter experts, existing systems, and previous efforts. This is naturally how the process starts and the work gets done. You will know when you have it right when the team relies less and less on these sources, and the requirements definition becomes the source of truth.

A requirements definition shall be explicit, precise, and concise

A requirements definition is not subject to interpretation. Its meaning is obvious. It explicitly states what needs to be stated, because there is no value in the implied. It should be written in terms that the business stakeholders understand, but still be approachable for those who are not subject matter experts. It should be free of undefined acronyms and jargon. It doesn't have to be a literary work of art, but it has to be well written. It does not have to be verbose. Terseness is a good thing, as long as the concepts are clear and complete.

A requirements definition shall be easily translated and traceable to the system design

For the requirements definition to be of real value, it must be readily translatable to the design of the system. When done well, the requirements definition, while not the design itself, will make the design obvious. It will become a key component of the system, providing context and explanation for the design, and ultimately for the implemented system. You will know you have it right when the requirements definition, in combination with the system design, is all that any stakeholder needs to fully understand the implemented system. Traceability of requirements through design and the implemented system is obvious. If in the end it is necessary for you to map the relationships between the requirements and the design in order to make them obvious, something has gone awry in your process.

Now that we know *what* requirements a requirements definition must satisfy, we can now safely engage in discussing a better way for *how* to create it.

7.
MODEL-DRIVEN
REQUIREMENTS ANALYSIS

In the field of IT, it is widely accepted that diagrams and pictures are very useful for quickly conveying ideas. The broad acceptance and use of such tools as Microsoft PowerPoint and Microsoft Visio makes this clear. But there is a big difference between drawing a picture and modeling. Without a standard notation that is widely understood and accepted, and without the underlying information (or metadata) that describes the picture, these artifacts are nothing more than arbitrary works of art. From project to project, analysts, architects, and developers, charged with preparing deliverables that describe the systems they plan to build, create pictures and diagrams to try to explain what they are thinking. Frequently, they make up their own symbols, or use semi-standard or standard symbols in novel ways. Unless they provide a legend describing what these symbols mean, which they never do, someone unfamiliar with the concepts and who was not directly involved in their creation, is left to interpret the meaning of these pictures and diagrams on their own. From person to person, no two interpretations will be the same. Further, each interpretation is guaranteed to be wrong and incomplete.

Model-driven requirements analysis, on the other hand, is a technique for surfacing, capturing and expressing the requirements of a system in a very rigorous and powerful way. Unlike traditional methods for expressing requirements, such as the widely-used list of "shall statements," model-driven requirements analysis is not only a technique for documenting requirements, but also a powerful means of facilitating discovery, creativity, and invention—the ultimate purpose of the analysis effort itself. Model-driven techniques are not only widely accepted in other fields such as architecture and engineering, they are practically the only techniques used in such fields. Model-driven techniques share some common characteristics.

First, they employ standard, widely-accepted notations. A notation, which includes symbology, meta-data definitions, and standards of use, provides a common language for expressing concepts. As an example, an architect prepares a set of plans that describes the design of a building. Though designs vary greatly from building to building, the plans that describe them are fairly similar. They will all include elevations, site plans, electrical plans, plumbing, structural plans, and so on. They use standard symbology that building contractors recognize and understand from one project to the next.

They are visual. For most of us, taking a thought or idea and forming a cohesive written statement to describe it is time consuming and relatively difficult. It is not uncommon for ideas to form and disappear faster than we can express them in writing. Drawing a picture, on the other hand, allows us to quickly articulate, explain, and capture an idea, and then set it aside for later with little loss in fidelity. It is true that a picture says a thousand words. If approached rigorously, visual methods are highly efficient.

Model-driven techniques enable and encourage logical simulation, or practice. They are about more than simply describing things, such as buildings, machines, or systems, they allow us to simulate them, and logically test them or practice with them before we actually build them. A model in this context is not the thing in miniature, but a logical simulation of the thing that allows us to visualize its realization. We use these models to mentally exercise and validate our ideas. A Unified Modeling Language (UML) sequence diagram is a good example. A developer will draw a sequence diagram in order to understand the behavior of a particular aspect of a system. In the process, he will uncover the subtleties and complexities that are easy to miss because our brains, during conversation, can easily gloss over these details and infer connections that don't really exist, without us even realizing it. During the activity of creating the sequence diagram, the developer is logically putting the system through its paces before actually building it.

Finally, model-driven techniques are tool enabled. You will be hard-pressed to find a model-driven technique that is not. Imagine architecture today without a tool such as AutoCAD. It's not that an architect couldn't design a building without the tool. It was done for centuries before such tools were available. But these days, it simply isn't practical to do this work by hand. It is far too labor-intensive, unproductive, and prone to error. The same is true for model-driven requirements analysis. Trying to do this work without the proper tool support is overwhelming and is abandoned in short order.

MODELING FOR CAPTURING REQUIREMENTS

For a model-driven approach to work at all, it must employ standard, widely accepted notations and modeling conventions. The Unified Modeling Language (UML) and Business Process Modeling Notation (BPMN) are two very mature modeling notations widely used in the field of information technology. They are intended to support the implementation of systems from project inception through the actual development of the software itself. As a result, they are very rich and fairly complex. To the uninitiated, just figuring out what models and diagrams to use can be daunting. But for the purpose of capturing requirements, it's pretty straightforward.

For requirements modeling, there are three models that we need to create. These models are highly interrelated and describe different aspects of systems requirements. Together they form a logical representation of the system to be. My purpose here is not to provide an exhaustive explanation of the UML and BPMN, but rather to explain these models: what they are, why we use them, the work involved in creating them, and the criteria used to determine their completeness. Along the way, I describe these models using the terminology that is inherent to the UML and BPMN. If you are completely new to these notations, this might be a little daunting, but keep in mind that the details of the modeling languages are not what matter at this point. It only matters that you understand the models themselves and the purposes that they serve, and that you begin to form a picture of the model-driven requirements process and how it facilitates creativity and invention.

Business Process Model

Business Process Models are the top-most layer of the logical models. The business process model is an important contextual model, describing from beginning to end who must do what in what sequence to accomplish the desired business outcome or outcomes. *Who* could be individual actors, organizational units, other organizations, or other systems. *What* includes any *task* that must be performed, manually or with the aid of some technology. It includes decisions that must be made, the passage of time (waiting), and *events* that trigger action. It also includes flows, which not only describe sequence, but can also describe the movement of materials or information into and out of the process as a whole, its subprocesses and tasks, or between systems and organizations. The standard notation for business process modeling is BPMN.

If the system you are defining is process-oriented, this model is absolutely necessary. It should be the model that you start with. At this point, it is entirely irrelevant if process automation technology is contemplated in the technology stack or not. Whether it is or isn't, the process will exist, and it needs to be defined. For systems that are not process-oriented, the process model may be useful, but it is not mandatory.

We create process models to provide the conceptual framework, or context, for the requirements definition as a whole. The process layer is the glue that holds the rest of the models together. It provides a clear boundary for the system. It informs the creation of the models that follow (the use case model and the domain model). In fact, these other models only exist to support and to provide additional detail for the process layer. For example, a use case should only exist in order to support some aspect of the process layer.

Process modeling helps us identify the participants in a process. It is a natural way to identify the major stakeholders in the system, as well as other systems that may be involved. You will name each participant with a noun and provide a brief description of each.

Process modeling allows us to identify the responsibilities of the process participants. In a process diagram, we assign each process participant to a *pool* or *lane*. Each task that must be performed in the process is placed in the lane of the participant responsible for performing it. In this way, we identify the responsibilities of the participants. You will provide a short, descriptive name for each task, starting with a verb. You will write a complete description of each task.

Process modeling helps us to identify the "sequence of events." Humans tend to think procedurally and sequentially. Though it is by no means the only way we need to think, for systems that are process oriented, it is necessary. And since we tend to be pretty comfortable with it, it's a great tool for making a lot of progress quickly. The line of questioning is easy, "What do I do first," and "what happens next?" The act of modeling this conversation will quickly reveal where we have missed something: a decision with only one outcome, a task with no out flow, not being able to follow a flow to a logical outcome, outcomes that are superfluous to our business objectives or that are counter to our objectives.

Finally, process modeling helps us to clarify the basic "contracts" between the participants. Where the process crosses the boundary from one participant to another, we know that we need to define the basic contract between them. When the participants are human actors, we think of this contract in terms of a supplier-customer relationship. We ask questions like, "John, as a supplier to Joe, what must you provide to him so that he can fulfill his role in the process?" and "Joe, as John's customer, what do you need from him in order to fulfill your role in the process?" These needs can include information (messages), or actual physical materials. Where one or both of the participants is another system, we think of these contracts as interfaces. At this point, we are not concerned with defining the details of these interfaces. It is enough to call out the nature of the information, or message, that needs to be exchanged (for example, "invoice," or "customer profile"). The details have a home elsewhere.

When the process models are complete, it should be obvious at a high level how the desired business outcome will be realized by the system. "System" in this context is used in the broadest sense, meaning people, process, and technology. If it is not obvious, then either the model is incomplete, or you have modeled the wrong thing.

Important elements in the model will be named and described. If you can't describe a participant, task, event, or message, your model is not complete. If you can't provide a description, then you aren't clear. And if you aren't clear, no one will be.

A subject matter expert who is a representative of a process participant, and who is reading the model should say "Yes! That's what we do," and should be able to clearly see how he or she affects, and is affected by, the process. The flow of the process will be clear. It will have a clear start and one or more clear outcomes.

The process model will consist of one or more diagrams. At a minimum, the highest-possible view of the process from end-to-end will be described in one diagram. One or more tasks in this diagram may represent sub-processes in the high-level process. These sub-processes will have diagrams of their own, as will sub-processes within sub-processes. This is known as *process decomposition*.

A key skill in process modeling is finding the right balance between diagram detail and process decomposition. A common tendency is to flatten the process into a single, massive, all-encompassing diagram that shows everything. The skill is in knowing when it is appropriate to define a sub-process for some portion of a larger process. Proper decomposition makes the process model much easier to follow and understand, as well as much easier to maintain. It can also help eliminate redundancy in the model when common process steps can be combined into reusable global processes.

If you find that a diagram has a very complex network of gates and flows, this is a good indication that you should look for ways to decompose it. If you find that you are either modeling the same process tasks across sub-processes, or are having to loop back to a series of tasks within a process, you likely have a sub-process that is common.

On the other hand, you can take process decomposition too far. A sub-process should only be defined if it orchestrates the execution of more than one use case. If the sub-process you are defining is limited to a single human actor and a system actor, or just a system actor, it's a good bet that you should model it as a use case (which I will describe next) instead of a sub-process. If a sub-process consists of only two or three tasks you should probably just include them in the parent process rather than create a sub-process.

Remember that the process model is not your only tool. Another common tendency is to try to describe everything in the process model. At this stage, the purpose of process modeling is not to design process automation. That may come later. You are not designing system interfaces, you are pointing out where they will be needed. You are not designing, or even describing user interfaces. That's what use cases are for. You are not designing data models or databases, you are simply calling out the logical entities that the process is acting on or using. At this point, you are inventing and capturing process, logically describing what the participants will do and how they will interact. These process definitions will inform many aspects of the system: operating procedures, work constructions, system architecture, and software design. But they are not, in and of themselves, any of these things.

Use Case Model

The UML Use Case Model is the next layer of the logical model. The use case arose from the realization that the traditional methods for gathering and organizing requirements were inadequate because they didn't emphasize enough the user's perspective of the system. Essentially, a use case is a *logical* unit of requirements for system functionality that allows an actor to accomplish some task. Think of it this way: rather than a pile of car parts, a use case describes an assembly, and how an actor will interact with that assembly. The actor could be a driver, a service technician, or another assembly. We don't have to concern ourselves with how that assembly will work, or how it will be built. We only have to concern ourselves with what it needs to do. In the design phase, we determine how a use case will be *realized* by various software elements (such as user interfaces, and methods on classes). Thus a use case ultimately represents something that we are going to build.

A use case allows us to describe logically how an actor will use the system to accomplish an outcome. We define use cases to provide structure to, and flesh out the details of, the functional requirements of the system. Everything that the system must do must ultimately be described in a use case. We model the functional requirements as use cases to ensure that we describe everything the system will do in terms of what the affected stakeholders care about. We explicitly call out what the stakeholders expect from each use case, especially if those interests conflict from one stakeholder to another. We call these expectations *stakeholder interests*. The outcome, or outcomes of a use case must satisfy the stakeholder interests. These outcomes are defined as *guarantees*. A guarantee describes the desired "state of the world" when the use case is complete. A *minimal guarantee* describes the absolute minimum that we expect from a use case. A *success guarantee* describes our desired result. The combination of the stakeholder interests and the guarantees define our *intent*.

Use case steps describe, step by step, how the actor will interact with the system in order to realize that intent. An actor can be a human or another system. Some path through the use case steps must lead to each minimal and success guarantee that has been defined for a use case. In this way, we describe how the desired outcomes are achieved, and thereby, how the stakeholder interests are satisfied. This not only helps to ensure that the requirements are complete, but also helps us to avoid unnecessary functionality and the unnatural acts that result from trying to satisfy extraneous or random functional requirements that just don't seem to fit or make sense. Think of these as the extra parts that you always seem to have after you have taken something apart and put it back together.

The use case is the least structured element within the UML and as a result, the most varied in application from project to project. This flexibility can come in handy, but without the imposition of some standards and guidelines, the effectiveness of the use case as a means for capturing and explaining requirements is limited. There is simply no way of knowing from client-to-client, project-to-project, or person-to-person, what you are going to get, and how it should be interpreted. Furthermore, the use case is often the most misapplied construct within the UML. Use cases tend to evolve into rambling textual descriptions of major chunks of solution functionality, with many requirements obscured within the content, and not fully described. The standard practice of describing use case steps in a purely textual outline form often results in pages of spaghetti pseudo code that is impossible to follow. This practice is dubious, especially given the modeling constructs within the UML at our disposal.

For example, the UML allows us to define something called an *activity*. We can associate an activity with a use case and name it "Use Case Steps." An activity can have a diagram, much like a process diagram. We can model each use case step as an *action* on the diagram. We can describe the sequence of steps by defining flows between the actions. You can even define *partitions*, which are synonymous with *lanes* in a process model to distinguish *who* does *what*. We can define two partitions, one for the primary actor and one for the system. We can show the actions taken by the primary actor, and the actions that the system takes in response. We can provide additional description to each of those actions as necessary. We can model alternative flows using control nodes which allow us to model branching, forking, merging, and so on.

The resulting activity diagram is a picture that says a thousand words. It will be much easier to follow than a purely written description. It will be richer and more complete. It will be more accurate because it is easy to see when we have missed something. Finally, it is simply easier and more efficient to do. We can think through the steps of the use case, modeling as we go. We can rearrange, reorder, add steps, and remove them until the end result works for us. It allows us to visually, rather than verbally, solve the puzzle.

A use case model will generally contain many use cases. Use cases that are logically related are grouped into *packages* that represent a logical category of requirements or functionality. For example, if we were describing the use cases for a car, we might have a package for "Power Train" or one for "Navigation." In this way, we not only define the structure of the use case model, but also take a big step toward logically organizing the system as a whole. A use case diagram is created in each package that shows the relationships between the use cases and their primary actors as well as their relationships to each other. For example, a use case may *include* other use cases, or be *extended* by other use cases. This allows us to visualize at a high level what the actors can do with the system. It also allows us to more easily visualize the scope of the system.

You will model use cases throughout the modeling effort, beginning sometime during the process modeling effort. While modeling the business processes, you will identify tasks that will require some interaction with the system, or in other words, software, to enable an actor to carry them out. These software-enabled tasks are use cases. You should capture them in the use case model as soon as you feel that the process model is reasonably stable. The process models will be your most obvious and richest source of use cases, but not your only source. For example, as the models mature, you will discover various administrative use cases, such as those required to maintain master data and and those required to enforce system security. The domain model (which I will describe next) will also be a source. Every entity in the domain model must ultimately originate from some use case.

When the use case model is complete, you will have created packages to organize the model into logical partitions that will ultimately reflect the organization of the system during design. Each package will have a description that summarizes and explains its contents. Think of a package as a section of a book, and the description as the introduction to the section. Each package will contain a use case diagram that shows the use cases in the package.

Each use case in the model will include a short, descriptive name. This name always starts with a verb. Each use case will also include a description which is usually brief, but can be as long as necessary to communicate what it needs to.

Any *preconditions* that must be true before the execution of the use case can begin will be defined. The logical execution of each use case will been described as use case steps. The steps start at the point that the preconditions have been met. They end when the guarantees have been met. They are absent of mechanism, and they are clear and understandable to all stakeholders.

The use case model demystifies the system, and allows us to wrap our minds around an enormous amount of detail without becoming overwhelmed. At a high level, we can quickly see everything that the system must do. We can then dive into the details of each use case in order to fully understand their intricacies and individual complexities. Back at the high level, we can see how the use cases work together. Now, we *really* understand. This is one of the beautiful things about modeling — all of those annoying and complex little details find a home, in the context of the whole, where they can be fully understood.

It is important to understand that creating a use case model is not just about writing up a bunch of use cases so that you write down some requirements and check off a deliverable. You are telling a story. You are describing what the system will be. You are painting a picture to help the stakeholders visualize the system and pace it with their imaginations. How you structure and organize this model is the key to accomplishing that result. Like any creative work of writing, how you organize the concepts and lay them out for the reader is the difference between good writing and bad, and between clearly communicating your message and not.

Domain Model

Like the foundation of a building, the domain model is the foundation for the other models. It is arguably the most important of all the models, not just for the requirements definition, but for many aspects of the implementation effort. And also like the foundation of a building, if you get it wrong, the rest doesn't matter much.

More than any other artifact, the domain model actually describes the business itself. The process models, use cases, and activity diagrams describe interactions, such as how actors interact with the various parts of the system, or how parts of the system interact with each other. But these interactions don't occur in a vacuum. They use, create, change, and destroy *things* in the system. The interactions themselves are meaningless outside of the context of these things. The domain model describes these "things of significance," which we call *entities*, that the actors act upon when using the system. It tells us what we need to know about those things, or their *attributes*. And it tells us how those things are related to each other and the nature of those relationships which we call *associations*. We model the domain using a UML class model.

Regardless of the type of system you are building, the domain model is a critical artifact. We model the domain so that we can gain a deep and nuanced understanding of the thing that we are dealing with, which for transformational efforts, is usually some aspect of a business enterprise. The domain lends context to everything else. It serves as a glossary, defining the *ubiquitous language* [1] that allows us to communicate effectively as a team. For those of us who are not subject matter experts (and even for those who are), it allows us to quickly grasp the structure and nature of the business domain (hence the name) from the perspective of the problem or opportunity that we are addressing. After a few days of working on the domain model, a team of people can be communicating remarkably effectively, even if a number of the team members have no prior experience with the domain.

The domain model lends tangibility to our efforts. Without the domain model, the processes that we model and the use cases that we define are simply too abstract to be truly meaningful. But with the domain model, these other models spring to life and become very precise as we begin to describe these interactions in terms of the real-world entities that they involve.

We model the domain so that we can understand the information requirements of the things that we will ask the system to do. In the old days, we used entity-relationship diagrams for this purpose, back when the principle objective of this activity was to inform database design. The domain model serves this purpose and much more. Later on in the effort, it will inform the design of the data persistence layer, whatever that may be, and the mechanisms for interacting with it. It will inform the design of the interfaces between systems. It will inform user interface design. But for the purpose of requirements definition the domain model allows us to understand and articulate the information requirements of the interactions that we have defined in terms of real-world things rather than database tables.

In addition to information we need to know about entities, the domain also allows us to describe the *behaviors* of entities. Think of behaviors as things that we can ask entities to do, or questions that we can ask them to answer. For example, I can ask the "Person" entity to tell me its age, which it can calculate based on its birthdate. I can ask the "Invoice" entity to tell me its total amount, which it knows by adding up the extended amounts of its line items, and then adding sales tax. I can also tell it to add or remove a line item. In the UML, behaviors are called *operations*. The concept of behavior can be a little hard to grasp at first. It helps if you think of entities as living things.

Identifying and assigning behavior to entities is a key activity of domain modeling because it allows us to find a home for requirements that don't naturally belong to just one, or any one single use case. This simplifies our efforts to describe processes and use cases. For example, if there are five use cases that require the total amount for an invoice, where do I describe how that amount is calculated? In the first one? In all of them? If I describe it in the first one, then I have to remember to look there when I need to refresh my memory on how it's done. If I describe it in all of them, I have to remember to update all five use cases if the requirements change. The domain model solves this problem. We can define the operation one time for the responsible entity (the "Invoice" entity in this example) where it naturally and intuitively belongs. That behavior is then available to any use case that requires it.

Domain modeling typically begins at the start of the modeling effort, whether that be process modeling or use case modeling, and continues throughout the requirements definition effort. The domain is usually the last model to be finished, as the use cases must be materially complete before we can be sure that the domain is complete. In reality, the domain model is very much a living document and will likely change and grow throughout the life of the system.

When the domain model is materially complete, every entity that is required by the use cases will be identified. Each will be named by a singular noun and will have a description that defines what it is as well as its significance to the system. Every entity will describe a real-world thing, something that a subject matter expert will readily recognize. The model will not include classes that describe purely technical constructs or software. The entities will be logically grouped into packages that represent major topics, or subject areas within the domain. This structure will inform the organization of the system during the design phase. All of the attributes for each entity will be named and described. The relationships between entities (their *association)* will be defined.

Domain modeling, even for the purpose of requirements definition, is fundamentally an activity of object-oriented analysis and design. A strong grasp of the principles and concepts of object orientation is required. A strong grasp of the UML, which is important for use case and activity modeling, is critical for domain modeling. Furthermore, it takes practice and experience to develop the necessary skills. Don't let this dissuade you. There is a wealth of resources at your disposal to learn this technique, including books, classes, training, and coaching. If your desire is to be a great business analyst or a great software developer, this is a key skill.

The really good news is that it is much easier to read and interpret a domain model than it is to actually create one. We have successfully taught hundreds of non-technical people (and technical people for that matter) to do it over the years. And by doing so, we have enabled them to communicate with us, with software developers, and even with each other, in an entirely new way — a way that is precise and succinct, that effectively bridges the gap between technologists and business people, and that translates seamlessly to software. Even so, it is almost guaranteed that at some point, someone will try to convince you that you shouldn't do it because it is beyond the grasp of non-technical people. I can't count the number of times that people have been shocked and dismayed to find out that, not only was I going to "waste time" creating a domain model, but that I was actually going to show the models to *business* people. Imagine their reactions when I told them that not only was I going to teach the business people to read the models, I was going to include them in the process of creating them as well!

From time to time, we run across business people that just don't have the patience for it, but generally people like it. It's puzzle-like, so it can be very engaging and kind of fun. It simplifies the conversation by relieving the subject matter experts of much of the burden of figuring out how to clearly articulate their ideas. All they have to do is answer questions and verify that those answers are properly represented in the model that is being created in front of them. It's much easier to say how the model is wrong, and even how to make it right, than it is to form, organize, and articulate a complete and cohesive concept on the fly.

If there is one thing that is painfully missing from the other methods for defining requirements, it's an effective means for describing the domain. In traditional requirements documents it is not uncommon to see the domain described as long lists of shall statements: "The system shall maintain information about customers," "the system shall maintain customer first name," "the system shall calculate total invoice amount," and so on; more car parts. Imagine if we tried to communicate the plans for a building in this manner. To say it would be ineffective would be the acme of understatement.

In other methodologies, since class modeling is considered to be far too technical for business people to understand, people rely on other mechanisms such as user interface and reports design to glean information requirements from the subject matter experts. But this is always ineffective because it prevents all of the project participants from gaining a complete and holistic view of the domain. The subject matter experts lose context of the whole because the conversation is limited to what they will see on a screen. The development team loses context of the whole because they have limited their understanding to snippets of interactions with the software and because they have excluded the subject matter experts from the conversation in general.

Remember that the work of defining the domain must be done one way or another. A model-driven approach makes the work of defining a good business domain model obvious, sometimes painfully so. This is not because a model-driven approach requires more effort. It simply makes clear the effort that is (and always has been) required. It takes patience and discipline, but the benefits include more engaged customers, more effective teams, higher-quality systems, and tremendous gains in productivity.

It is useful to think of the business process model, the use case model, and the domain model as layers of a larger system model. Like the different plans in an architectural drawing, these models build upon each other to logically describe the system as a whole. The process models identify the major participants, what they will do, and how they will interact. They will help us to identify when these participants will need software to perform their tasks. These tasks become use cases, the next layer down. And underpinning it all, like a foundation plan, is the structural model, or domain. We can now take a representative business scenario and step-by-step, logically walk it through these models to simulate how the system will behave. Taken as a whole, we now know everything we need to know in order to design the physical system.

In the design process, additional models can be added to describe the physical design of the system, such as architectural models, collaborations, class models to describe software, sequence diagrams to describe interactions between architectural or software components, and so on. But unlike the architectural drawings of a building, these models can be used to actually create the physical product. The logical models can be used to generate requirements documentation. They can be transformed into design models. Design models can be used to generate design deliverables. And best of all, they can be used to generate actual software. By modeling the system in sufficient detail, you are not only fully describing it, you are actually starting to build it. And all of those other documents that you have to deliver but hate to produce? You get those for free!

MODELING FOR CREATION AND INVENTION

Capturing requirements is one thing. But bringing them to the surface to begin with is quite another. Consider how we typically attack the problem. Business analysts and subject matter experts are chosen for their subject matter expertise derived from experience within the organization or experience on similar projects. Why is that? It should be because their experience and knowledge will inform the process of invention. But really it's because of the tacit belief that they already know what needs to be done.

The fact is that on teams that are comprised of consultants and client subject matter experts, what is known of the problem domain is always less than 100 percent, and usually much less. Consultants (if we are lucky) know maybe 20 percent of what is necessary, and subject matter experts know maybe 80 percent. Consultants, of course, would like to believe that the situation is reversed, and everyone would like to believe that they know all that needs to be known to accomplish the goal. But the reality is quite different. Everyone has something to learn.

Experience in a particular problem domain is very useful of course, but it also burdens us with assumptions and expectations. An over-reliance on experience can cause us to assume that certain aspects of the problem domain, and therefore of the solution, are implied. But there is no value in the implied, because that which is implied may be wholly misunderstood, understood vastly differently from one person to the next, or missed entirely. The assumption that everyone "gets the basics" causes us to gloss over much of the problem domain out of fear of wasting time.

An over-reliance on experience can cause us to assume that we already fully understand the problem domain, and in fact, expect that we do. This expectation causes us to advocate strongly for our beliefs, rather than engage in dialog in order to truly understand. It causes us to not explore issues deeply, out of fear of wasting time, and out of fear that we may appear to not be the experts. It limits the scope of our creativity to what we already know.

An over reliance on the experience of others (experts) causes us to accept inadequate or inappropriate solutions. Rather than strive for deep understanding and then for a truly meaningful solution, we accept "patterns," or we attempt to repeat something that we or someone else has done before, or we rely on "best practices." What we are really doing is being intellectually lazy in the name of expediency.

Essentially, we approach the requirements analysis process as if the requirements are already known and out there, and that all we have to do is write them down in an organized way. This could not be further from reality. The requirements don't exist, because the solution must be invented. It is intuitive, but incorrect, that we must first understand the requirements before we can invent the solution. What is counter-intuitive but true is that once we have completed the effort of invention, the requirements will be understood. The ability to create and invent as a team throughout the project life cycle is the single most important factor for successful transformational efforts. The requirements analysis phase is not only when the process of creation and invention begins, it's when 80 percent of it happens. The real power that model-driven requirements analysis brings to bear, and truly its real value, is how it super-charges the process of creation and invention.

We don't typically associate creativity with the field of information technology, or business in general for that matter. But the most important part of our job is to create. And we are required to do so on demand. We don't have the luxury of staring out the window with our feet on the desk until inspiration finds us. We must *invoke* inspiration. Model-driven requirements analysis provides us a structured means of invoking inspiration and creating predictably.

Structure and creativity may seem like incompatible constructs until you understand how it works. First, we know from the start the final form that the creative product must take. And not in the way a songwriter knows that the end product will be a song, or a painter knows that the end product will be an oil painting. We actually know what the end product must contain. We may be starting with a blank canvas, but we will structure our creation and fill the canvas the same way, every time. Second, we know the steps we need to take to fill the canvas. If we are disciplined in taking those steps, we know that the canvas will be filled. Third, we aren't individual artists waiting for creative ideas to pop into our heads. We are surfacing, clarifying, and completing the ideas that are already in our heads, and combining them with everyone else's. A natural by-product of this synthesis of ideas is the emergence of entirely new ones.

The process looks something like this: you stand up, walk over to the board and grab a marker. On one part of the board you start drawing a process model. Step-by-step, you work through the process. Who does what? What happens next? On another part of the board, you start drawing a class model, as the entities (nouns, "things of significance") emerge in the conversation. On another part of the board, you will start a use case model, drawing actors and use cases as the tasks emerge that will require the aid of software to perform (for example, "Create an Invoice"). You will move easily from one model to the other, all the while explaining the constructs that you are using and how to interpret them. You will focus on a particular model as long as it is productive to do so, and move on when it is not. Before you know it, board after board will be filled, photographed, erased, and filled again.

Something happens along the way. When you start the meeting, what you see on people's faces ranges from sheer boredom to anxiety and even outright irritation. As you begin, some people are listening, others are answering emails and texts. The first shift begins when you stand up and walk to the board. People automatically pay more attention to a person standing before them. Then you start asking questions and drawing the answers on the board in the form of models. Now it becomes a puzzle and it is tangible to them, not just random conversation. People love puzzles and as the process picks up momentum, the next shift happens. The expressions of boredom, fear, and irritation evaporate, replaced by curiosity. People sit up in their chairs. Their phones and email are forgotten. They are actively participating and what they are saying is appearing on the board before them where they can evaluate it, adjust it, and move on because they don't have to hold all the details in their heads. The little details that are important to them find a home in the context of the story that is emerging before them. They debate, even argue, but ultimately, all is resolved in the models. The models help them to clarify competing ideas, try them out, accept them or reject them.

And then, if things go really well (which they often do), someone else is compelled to stand up and come to the board. It might be a subject matter expert or an architect or a developer. You hand her the pen and sit down. Now the real magic happens. As she works to express what she is thinking, others will get up and join her at the board. There will often be two or three people at the board at any given time. Your job is to keep the conversation on track, help them with modeling their ideas, and help them get unstuck from time to time. You will moderate debates and contribute your own ideas when it seems relevant. But it is no longer your meeting. It is everyone's meeting. And things will be happening fast. People will get excited. You'll have to keep them focused and keep it to a single conversation. This means that you will have to listen to the side conversations that erupt, and know when to either hold them aside or bring them to the main conversation. The time will fly by and people will be genuinely surprised when the meeting time comes to an end.

It's exhausting work. People can do it productively for maybe four to six hours at a time at the most. Once people get tired, they get stuck and they get frustrated. Or they simply can't focus. That's when you have to call it a day. It may only be 2 o'clock in the afternoon. That's ok. Go get a bite to eat and just talk. You will be amazed at the amount of work that actually gets accomplished that way.

You might do this for a day or two and then you have to stop and formally capture and document what you have. This intellectual break in the action is important for two reasons. First, ideas take time to mature. Though you won't be working together as a team, it is guaranteed that everyone will still be thinking — turning the questions over in their minds, consciously or subconsciously. Very often, you will see a surge of clarity and creativity when a team gets back together after a break. Second, as an analyst, you need some alone-time to think. As you begin to formally build the model, you will uncover the holes and the questions. Many of these you will resolve yourself, simply because the activity of modeling will make it clear to you what needs to be done. Others you will note for later and these will be the starting point for the next team conversation. When you have captured, documented, and clarified everything that you can, it's time to meet again.

In the next meeting, you begin by reviewing what you have captured in the models. This is the group's opportunity to see the formal result of the effort, as well as your opportunity to validate the thinking so far. Problems, holes, and questions will be revealed. You will adjust and clarify the models as a team. In this process, the models become tangible and legitimate. What were once nascent, fragile ideas are now concrete, common understanding. Now you can press on and continue to expand and build on this understanding.

And so the process goes. In the first few meetings you are looking for the boundaries to ensure that you have identified the scope of what needs to be defined. This will become obvious and the team will make conscious choices about what is in and what is out. After that, it is simply a matter of driving to the details. Are all process details described? Are all use cases "fully dressed," with descriptions, preconditions, stakeholder interests, guarantees, and steps? Are all entities and attributes described? There will come a point when all that is known and knowable is defined. Everybody will recognize it. And you will know that you are finished. Now it's time to build something, because there is nothing more to learn until we do.

At this point, the elaboration of requirements is complete to the degree necessary to support the design and construction of the system. But the models are by no means finished. They will continue to change. If 80 percent of the invention happens during the elaboration of requirements, the remaining 20 percent happens during design and build. And it's the hard 20 percent. The team will uncover problems, gaps, and hidden complexities. The models must change in order to resolve the problems, close the gaps, and clarify the complexities.

This is natural and good. As hard as we try, we can't think of everything up front. We can't really know until we actually *prove it*. As we incorporate this learning, our invention becomes more rational and robust and as a result, so do our requirements. This idea might make you uncomfortable. Yes, the requirements can and must change during design and build. The notion that requirements are immutable after the requirements phase is complete is silly. It ignores the reality of the very human process of learning and it implies that project pressures are more important than new knowledge. Of course, we must always be pragmatic and balance new learning with the need to deliver the product, but we do that together, as a team, with the full knowledge that nothing is more important than a successful outcome.

Once mastered, this discipline is unmatched for the acquisition of a shared understanding. The efficiency of this process and the quality of the outcome are unparalleled. Until you have experienced it for yourself, it's a little hard to believe. The requirements definition is more clear, and far more complete. More than just a set of deliverables, the result is a collective consciousness across the team around the desired outcomes and what needs to be done to achieve them. And you will get there much faster than by any other means.

This drives tremendous productivity gains throughout the project life cycle in many ways, some obvious and some not. For example, design and build go much faster. There is less guesswork. It's more productive because the requirements are clear and more complete from the start. There are fewer missed requirements and fewer defects. Quality assurance and user acceptance testing take less time, not only because there are fewer defects, but also because it is easier to define how the system should be tested. The acceptance criteria are more clear.

With the proper tooling, even greater productivity gains can be achieved. Formal deliverables documents can be published from the models themselves, meaning that once the models are complete, the deliverables can be produced at the push of a button. As the models change, the documents are simply regenerated. If during the analysis process it is discovered that the models need to be fundamentally reorganized or changed, reorganizing the document is again simply a matter of pushing a button. The activity of modeling is the real work. The deliverables are a by-product.

Notes

1.   Evans, Eric. *Domain-Driven Design: Tackling Complexity in the Heart of Software.* Addison-Wesley, 2003. p. 24-30.

8.
ADOPTING
A MODEL-DRIVEN DISCIPLINE

M odel-driven techniques are nothing new in the field of IT. They have been around in one form or another for decades. The advent of formal notations, such as the Unified Modeling Language (UML) and Business Process Modeling Notation (BPMN), has provided us with rich and expressive visual and textual modeling languages for describing solution requirements. Still, there is a fundamental misunderstanding of what constitutes a truly useful requirements definition and how to apply these notations and techniques to achieve that result. While the "shall statement" won't die despite its obvious ineffectiveness, model-driven techniques struggle to gain ubiquitous acceptance despite their obvious and seemingly widely understood value.

There are a number of contributing factors. First, it takes some effort to learn how to apply model-driven techniques. The notations themselves have to be learned and mastered. Both the UML and BPMN are wide and deep. They overlap to some degree but are also targeted to specific purposes, which can be confusing. Some conventions of the notations are well suited to capturing requirements and others are specific to design and implementation. Learning what models and diagrams to use and how to create and organize them takes study and practice. The tools that are used to do it tend to be complicated and take time to master. Just choosing a tool from the many available options is daunting, because until you know what you need it's hard to tell which tools will meet your needs and which won't.

Second, it is a completely different paradigm for capturing requirements from what most people are familiar with. Analysts not only have to get comfortable themselves with doing it, but also with explaining to their target audience how to read and interpret the work product. They have to be willing to deal with some resistance in this process. Other team members will be resistant because the process will feel uncertain and the deliverables will be unfamiliar. They will likely apply tremendous pressure to revert to "what works," which really means "what we're used to."

Finally, it feels highly unproductive to move up this learning curve. It gets easier and goes faster the more times you do it, but at first it feels awkward and uncertain mostly because it's new. In short, it takes no small amount of conviction and dedication to adopt these techniques.

The good news is that there are ways to ease the transition so that it really doesn't have to be that hard. With some guidance and focused intention, this transition can be made with no loss of productivity. In fact, you can experience significant improvements in productivity and quality very quickly.

The first step is to learn the standard notations. For business process modeling, the standard notation is Business Process Modeling Notation. For use case modeling and domain modeling the standard notation is the Unified Modeling Language. These notations are well known and widely accepted. Every real modeling tool available implements them. They have been developed over years of effort by many talented people so they are very mature, rich, and expressive. The Object Management Group is the standards organization that is the steward of these notations. They offer a wealth of information and training. Additionally, there are literally hundreds of books and online resources at your disposal.

Begin by simply studying the notations to familiarize yourself with them. Focus on the basics. Both notations are very deep, but there is plenty within both that can be deferred for later, or safely ignored. They both contain a good deal of information regarding their theoretical and structural underpinnings, which is interesting if you are a modeling geek, but not particularly useful for your immediate purposes. For the UML, start with the basics of class modeling, use case modeling, and activity diagramming. Additionally, study the basic principles of object oriented analysis and design. For BPMN, study the basics of process modeling. For both, as you learn to use them you will discover how and when to apply their more subtle conventions in circumstances where they will simplify your models and make them more expressive. Remember that this is always your goal. It's easy to get carried away at showing your command of the notations at the expense of expressiveness and simplicity.

Practice with the notations on topics you already know well. This will teach you to express yourself in these new languages. Pick a process that you already understand and model it. Take a stab at identifying and modeling the use cases within it. Model the domain that is represented. In this exercise, be sure to stick to the standard symbols and conventions of the notations. Making it up is not allowed. You can do it on a white board, on paper, or using a diagramming tool like Microsoft Visio. Once you feel like your models make sense, review them with someone else. This will teach you to talk through your models in front of people. It will show you where you rely too much on verbal explanation rather than on the models themselves to communicate your story. It will hone your skills with the notations. It won't take too many iterations of this before your command of the notations will be sufficient to do it for a real project.

There is no substitute for practice, so jump in as soon as possible. Your results may not be perfectly modeled, but that doesn't matter. As long as you are improving the level of clarity and understanding across the team, it's good enough. At this stage in the learning process, you are simply conducting the conversation in a different way. Your results will be far better and more useful than if you are not doing it at all.

Modeling by hand or with a diagramming tool will only get you so far. You need to find a good modeling tool and learn to use it fairly early in the learning process. Without a modeling tool that will allow you to capture not only your diagrams but also the details behind them — and to add to them and update them easily — the diagrams that you draw will quickly get shoved aside to gather dust in the corner. Their usefulness will be limited to driving the initial conversation.

There is a big difference between drawing a diagram and modeling. A diagram is not a model. It is a view into a model. The details that you capture about the diagram, its meta-data, is where its real usefulness lies. This is what turns a picture into a model. A diagramming or drawing tool will enable you to create the picture, but it won't enable you to capture its details. You will be forced to capture and maintain the details in other documents or to try to capture all of the details on the diagram itself. This will become overwhelming as soon as the models grow to any significant size. Keeping the diagrams and their related information in sync will become very difficult, and too inefficient to justify. If you try to capture all the details on the diagrams themselves, they will be too dense visually to follow and just as impossible to maintain.

These are very common problems that consistently undermine people's efforts at model-driven disciplines. As in any craft, the proper tools are critical. There are a number of good modeling tools available. When choosing one for the purposes of model-driven requirements analysis, there are a few key features that you need to look for. Besides providing diagramming capabilities, a good tool will function as a repository for your models and will allow you to organize them (and reorganize them) as you see fit. It will allow you to capture the details of the model elements within it. Any tool that faithfully implements the UML or BPMN will allow this. And finally, a good modeling tool will provide at least some capability for publishing. This is very important, because unless you can present the contents of your models in a manner that is consumable by other stakeholders who are not using the tool, the usefulness of your models will be severely limited.

For a business analyst, developing strong facilitation skills is mandatory. This is true regardless of how you elicit requirements. But when using a model-driven discipline, the skills required are somewhat different. You have to learn to use the process of modeling to drive the conversation in a meaningful and productive way. A prerequisite is a strong command of the notations and the techniques. But additionally, facilitating a model-driven conversation requires that you get up in front of the room and take command.

This isn't optional. First, you have to seize control. This isn't as easy as it sounds. It is uncommon for someone to stand up in a regular meeting and take command. Once people know you and know your style, it's easy. But in a new group, it can feel very awkward. It is a learned skill to be able guide the conversation to the point where you can grab the marker and step up to the board in front of the room.

Once you are there, you have to run the room. To do this, you have to learn how to ask the questions that will start the conversation. Getting started is the hardest part. Once the models start to form, the conversation will take on a life of its own, but you have to get to that point. The key is to pull the conversation back to the simplest, highest-level starting point possible. One way to do this is to ask the room a question like, "Tell me, in one sentence starting with a verb, what we are trying to do with this system?" The answer will of course be different in every situation, but it should be simple, like "Adjudicate an insurance claim," or "Treat a patient." You will be surprised by how often this question is hard to answer. It's a great exercise for engaging the group and starting the conversation in a meaningful way. The next question will be, "What do we have to do to do this? How does it start? Where does it end?" And now you are off and running.

If that approach seems inappropriate, or doesn't work, another approach is to ask the individuals in the room to tell you their top three biggest concerns regarding the effort they are about to undertake. This will certainly get people talking, and it is a great way to surface problems or issues that are not obvious and to bring people's fears into the open. This exercise will reveal to you key points on which you can hang the conversation, at least to get started. At some point early in almost every effort, you should go through this exercise if for no other reason than to get people used to the idea and the process of revealing themselves in a more intimate way.

You have to learn to read the people in the room. It is important to recognize when people are confused, concerned, irritated, or desperate to say something. If anyone in the room is struggling to grasp a concept, you have to see that and slow the conversation down to bring that person along. If someone is concerned, you have to read that and direct the conversation to help that person articulate that concern so that it can be addressed. People are conditioned to not speak up. Most people aren't practiced at expressing themselves. Instead, they are resigned to being quiet, frustrated, and irritated. If you are out of your own head enough to pay attention, you will see these emotions in the faces of the people in the room. Some people are harder to read than others, but engaging them is remarkably straight-forward. It's simply a matter of stopping and asking something like, "I see that there is something bothering you. Are we missing something?"

On the other hand, you sometimes have to gently shut down someone who is over-dominant in the room. This person will have trouble letting other people talk, will cut them off, and in the worst cases, will bully others into not talking. It's your job to ensure that the conversation remains balanced. It is usually just a matter of saying something like, "Hold on a second; I want to hear what he has to say."

There are many other subtle skills that you will learn. Once people get comfortable and figure out the rules of engagement, your challenge will be to keep every one from talking at once. You will learn when to let people run amuck and blow off steam. You will learn when you need to call it quits for the day. And all the while, with all of this highly dynamic interaction going on, you will be capturing the outcomes of this conversation at the board in process diagrams, use cases, and class diagrams.

Besides learning to facilitate, you must also learn to participate. It sounds easy, but as consultants we are conditioned to feel that we have to do all the talking: the person who says the most words wins. After all, that's what experts do, right? But if you are doing it right you are listening as much as you are talking and probably more. Even as the facilitator, if you are participating properly you will interject what you have to say into the conversation, not as the sage at the front of the room but as a colleague. As a participant it is your responsibility to ensure that *you* understand. That means that you will ask as many questions as you need to until you are clear and really get it, even when everyone else in the room seems to already understand and even if the questions seem stupid.

If you do this, especially as the facilitator, it gives everyone else in the room permission to do it as well. The degree that this is required varies from situation to situation. Some groups of people are more relaxed and comfortable with these kinds of conversations than others. But in any case, the goal is clarity. The permission to do whatever it takes to achieve it is very important. It is not possible to achieve clarity as a group until the individuals themselves are clear.

Finally, a key skill is recognizing when to hand the reins over to someone else. This is important both for keeping the conversation as productive as possible and for keeping the group engaged. For example, there are times when someone else in the room is better suited to lead the conversation because he or she possesses special knowledge or experience about the topic at hand. Or there will be times when a participant is struggling to explain something to you (or you're struggling to understand) and you hand that person the pen and say, "show me." And best of all there will be times when a flash of clarity strikes someone in the room and that participant will be dying to take over.

This is an organic, boot-strap approach to getting started with a model-driven process. It is a necessary first step for building personal and organizational knowledge and acceptance. But this will only take you so far. Eventually, you will need to make the transition to a more formal, scalable, and industrialized process. When the time comes that you want to make that transition, find a coach. The wholesale adoption of a model-driven process is not a trivial effort. Tools must be purchased or built, processes developed, and people trained. People will need hands-on help to get their work done while learning along the way. The organizational change is significant and must be navigated with patience and care. A coach (which could be a person or an organization) can help you with the heavy lifting, save you a lot of time on key decisions, and keep you out of the minefields. There is nothing that will make this transition easy, but a good coach will save you a lot of time, money, and pain along the way.

9.

BATTLING SELF-DECEPTION

"Commitment to the truth does not mean seeking the Truth, the absolute final word or ultimate cause. Rather, it means a relentless willingness to root out the ways we limit or deceive ourselves from seeing what is, and to continually challenge our theories of why things are the way they are."

PETER M. SENGE [1]

Shared understanding is profoundly important to clarity, but it is by no means all that there is to it. Throughout the project life-cycle, a discipline of clarity also requires us to be clear-eyed about our current reality in relation to where we want to be, especially when our reality isn't so great. As a team and individually, we must be willing to acknowledge our problems, weaknesses, and challenges so that we can address them and move forward. In his book *Good to Great,* Jim Collins describes this quality as the Stockdale Paradox:

*"You must maintain unwavering faith that you can and will prevail in the end, regardless of the difficulties, AND **at the same time** have the discipline to confront the most brutal facts of your current reality, whatever they might be."*[2]

Transformational efforts by nature are difficult and problematic. Every project will have its problems and sometimes they will be severe. Within the context of transformational efforts, the Stockdale Paradox is characterized by an unwavering commitment to a successful outcome above all else and the faith that you will be successful in the end, while at the same time having the discipline to face the brutal facts of the current situation. The brutal fact might be that you are hopelessly over budget or behind schedule. It might be that there is something you really must do that will put you over budget or behind schedule. It might be that you missed something big and important in the requirements. It could be that you made a poor design choice. The list is essentially endless. What matters most isn't the nature of the problem, but how you respond to it.

Unfortunately, self-deception is the easier road and the one most frequently traveled. It is easier and less painful in the moment to sweep a problem under the rug and hope that it goes away than to acknowledge it and deal with it head on. Far too often, we respond by ignoring the problem or denying it. Or worse, we respond in a way that will shield ourselves at the expense of others or at the expense of the overall success of the project. The signal that this is happening is when other things become more important than a successful outcome: A deadline, a budget, a signed-off requirements document, the next contract. This is another point where the discipline of trust and the discipline of clarity intersect, and an example of why trust is a prerequisite for clarity. If we trust each other and we all know that we can rely on each other to do what is best, it's much easier for any one person to hit the stop button. It allows us to acknowledge and face trouble together without blame and to do whatever it takes to preserve a successful outcome.

This by far is the hardest part of the discipline of clarity. No one wants to be the bearer of bad news, the one to blame, the one to hold up progress, the one who is "the problem." No one, except for maybe the adrenaline junky, really wants to expose themselves to the risk of raising their hand. It can be very tricky to confront people with the facts in environments where people have little experience or discipline in facing them. The truth will not be welcome. People get scared and then they get angry. They will feel betrayed somehow, even though you are doing nothing to betray them. They may turn on you. We do our best to lead people to their own conclusions rather than beat them over the head with reality. But there are times when it is simply unavoidable. This usually happens when we are being asked to go along with some self-deceiving decision or behavior that is guaranteed to cause serious trouble down the road.

One time we were working for a software company on a proof of concept using their manufacturing scheduling system. The client was a large biotech company with a very complex manufacturing process and severe scalability constraints. They really needed to squeeze every bit of capacity out of their plant as possible. We worked on it for a significant amount of time and after a tremendous amount of effort and some enhancements to the underlying software product, we were able to make it work. The problem was that to satisfy the entire manufacturing problem, the software required further enhancement at significant cost to the client. Additionally, we estimated that the consulting effort to fully implement the software would be very large and very costly.

The client was not happy. They had sought to purchase a packaged application precisely to avoid the cost and risk of building their own. They did not want a heavily-customized product. In their thinking, it defeated the purpose of purchasing a packaged application. They were particularly unhappy about the estimated cost of implementation. How could it cost *that much* to implement a purchased piece of software? They had spent a significant amount of money and time on the proof of concept. I suspect that from their point of view, we were simply pressing our advantage in order to extract as much money out of them as we possibly could.

The reality was that their problem was extremely complex and was going to take significant effort and resources to solve, regardless of how they chose to solve it. Further, until we had completed the work required to understand this, there was no way for any of us to know. It was never our intent to deceive them. We had simply clarified the facts, and the facts were not good.

The product development team and the software sales people sensed defeat. The head of the sales organization came in to save the deal. Naturally, one of the first items to come under attack were the implementation estimates. By this point, we understood the problem well. We knew how hard it had been to get the proof of concept operational. We knew what was left to do to fully solve the problem. A very large part of the estimated effort was the modeling required to acquire a shared understanding. We knew, due to the complexity of the manufacturing processes and the complexity of the recipes, that there were many subtle nuances and unknowns that we were bound to uncover, and that these would have a significant impact on the design and the implementation.

It soon became clear that the client was not going to buy the product. There was really no benefit in terms of cost, risk, or ongoing support in purchasing the software over building a custom solution. The sales executive and the product manager were desperate to save the deal. We came under intense pressure. During one conversation, the sales executive asked if we really had to do all of "that requirements analysis and modeling." The product manager said "no."

For us, the acquisition of a shared understanding is not negotiable. How we acquire it is also not negotiable. As the conversation continued, it was simply assumed that we would abandon what we normally do in favor of a "faster way," and that we could therefore significantly reduce our cost estimates and the deal might be saved. I literally had to interrupt the conversation to say that there was no way we were going to do that, and if that's what they wanted to do, they would do it without us.

One of my biggest fears is that I will get pushed into a situation where I am guaranteed to fail. This has happened enough times that my discomfort with this possibility far outweighs my discomfort with putting my foot down and dealing with the problem in the moment. But it is still uncomfortable, and this discomfort makes me edgy, even angry. I will almost always come across harsher in those moments than is useful. I could have been more patient and picked a better time. I could have taken my time to explain our position. But these are the personal challenges of the discipline of clarity. Once again, that's why we call it a *discipline*.

What do these battles look like? Project management battles over timelines and estimates. Being ordered to do things that were not only nonsensical and wildly unproductive, but also damaging to the final outcome. Being told to alter the requirements since they had to be wrong because some aspect of the chosen solution wouldn't support them. For years, I felt utterly powerless in these situations. After all, I was being paid to do as I was told, right?

Wrong! I was being paid to solve a problem. I was being paid to do *everything I could* to deliver a successful outcome. I came to understand that my only leverage in these situations was to simply say, "No." It is never easy, but the vast majority of the time, it is simply a matter of working through it. It is sort of an awareness-denial-anger-bargaining-acceptance type of cycle. But in rare and extreme situations, it really can get ugly. You will invoke more of a fight-or-flight response.

It is in these situations that *you* have to face the brutal facts of your situation: "There is nothing more I can do for these people. I can no longer help them." In my experience, these are excruciatingly frustrating moments. There is no worse feeling than that of throwing in the towel. It means defeat. But remember that you have only three choices. I have made all three. You can walk away gracefully and find the next great thing to do. You can pretend that you can still win, and suffer the grinding, heartbreaking, slow and bitter decline that ends in total failure. Or you can acknowledge that the ship is sinking, ride it down for all it's worth, and hope you catch a lifeboat before it goes completely under. This is risky, and a waste of time and spirit. It is just another way of shifting the burden. Remember that it is your choice to *invest* your time productively or to *spend* it. The more disciplined you are about this choice, the more you will grow, the more successful you will be, the more opportunities you will have, the more freedom you will have to choose how you will invest your time.

Notes

1.   Senge, Peter M. *The Fifth Discipline: The Art and Practice of the Learning Organization*. Rev. and updated ed. New York: Doubleday/Currency, 2006. p. 31.

2.   Collins, Jim. *Good to Great: Why Some Companies Make the Leap...And Others Don't* HarperBusiness, 2011. iBooks. https://itun.es/us/yhVOA.l.

PART 3:
THE DISCIPLINE OF PROCESS

Because the ability to learn, create, and innovate is critical to success, it cannot be left to chance. It must be predictable. It is tempting to think that this ability occurs only as a happy accident created by the mix of just the right people, working on just the right project at just the right time; that successful results are random and unpredictable. If this is the case, as it often is, we have little chance of success. The key to predictability is discipline in process. That means putting in place processes that are proven to work and having the discipline to follow them *relentlessly*. Discipline in process is our weapon against uncertainty.

Beyond our need to facilitate learning there is also the reality that we simply cannot afford the time or the risk associated with inefficient "make-it-up-as-you-go" activities. Neither do we have time for the slavish devotion to overbearing and unwieldy methodologies that accomplish nothing more than to fool ourselves into believing that we are mitigating our process risk. A process discipline cannot be achieved simply by defining a procedure and a list of required deliverables. A discipline of process is more like a lifestyle choice. It is as much a culture and a philosophy as it is a formal set of methods, processes, tools, and deliverables. It is almost impossible to force and to enforce. To say it must be embraced is not quite strong enough — that implies that there is a conscious value judgment or acceptance. Rather, a discipline of process is embedded and lived, inseparable from all that we do and how we do it. It underlies all aspects of successful transformational efforts.

10.
PRINCIPLES OF GOOD PROCESS

As an industry we lament our poor results, yet we rarely follow our own processes with anything resembling discipline. And to make matters worse the processes we *aren't* following tend to be pretty bad to begin with. Commonly accepted practices in the industry today generally emphasize the wrong things or not enough of the right things. For many years, the industry has chased lower hourly rates at the expense of everything else, and in particular, productivity and quality.

To begin with, our widely accepted processes are geared more toward protecting ourselves from each other than toward achieving a successful outcome. Our processes are burdened by the silly, non-productive, energy-wasting activities that we are forced to include in order to protect ourselves from each other: tedious, protracted review cycles, formal sign-offs, ridiculous change processes, arduous documentation. We end up spending more time in meetings, arguing the most minute details, than we do actually working. This is where the discipline of trust and the discipline of process intersect. Without trust, it is difficult to implement truly effective processes. Since trust is the exception rather than the rule, ineffective processes are commonly applied and generally accepted.

For example, we produce a requirements document and make the business stakeholders sign it. Later, if we learn something and determine that the requirements are wrong or incomplete, we can hold them accountable for missing it. Does it matter if the requirements document was any good to begin with? Not really, because most of the time it isn't. We torture and coerce them into signing. We make them sit through long, tedious meetings for weeks, with no end in sight. We hand them thick, incomprehensible documents and give them five days for review and comment. If they are uncomfortable with the requirements there will be more meetings and requested changes. Then more reviews and maybe more changes. If this happens more than a couple of times, we begin to complain that the business people have no idea what they want. We begin to feel righteous about pressuring them. After all, they are holding up the project. Whether they are comfortable or not, we demand their approval, "We are awaiting your approval and cannot move forward until we receive it. The project timeline is at risk." Sign it or else! And they do.

The lower the trust, the worse it gets. Next come the painstakingly detailed meeting minutes so that we will have something to wave in each other's faces later. Then, the first time someone denies that something was actually said, the meeting minute reviews and sign-offs begin. And so it goes. The machinery slowly grinds to a halt.

Commonly accepted processes tend to be inspection focused. We attempt to inspect quality into the output, rather than designing processes that produce quality output to begin with. We review, review, and review. We test, test, and test. But our quality improves very little. This is because the big problems can't be corrected without starting over and most of the problems we manage to detect are superficial. Our timelines lengthen. Since we only have so much time for rework, we eventually have to give up. In the end, we are forced to abandon the process for the sake of getting *something* done. Poor quality is systemic.

My favorite example of quality by inspection is the Requirements Traceability Matrix (RTM). Its stated purpose is to ensure that all requirements are implemented. It starts with a list of requirements in the form of a truckload of car parts. It should be simple, right? The developers are delivered the parts and all they have to do is base their design on the requirements. Everything they need to know is in the pile. Then it is simply a matter of building according to the design. Later, we can trace our requirements to the implementation by putting together the requirements traceability matrix. By doing so, we ensure that every requirement is implemented: quality by inspection.

This process assumes that the requirements are complete and understandable. It assumes that their interpretation is inherently common and uniform. It assumes that all of the requirements are rational and will map neatly and coherently to some physical aspect of the implementation. *None* of these assumptions are valid. Therefore, the requirements traceability matrix is pointless. No amount of review and inspection will change the fact that this process is deeply flawed to begin with.

Worse yet are the silly things we do next. The hours of meetings trying to find homes for requirements that have none. Pointless, expensive changes to designs and software made to accommodate random, senseless requirements — those left-over nuts and bolts. Not only did we waste our time to begin with, we reduced the quality of our product as well.

Commonly accepted practices tend to be task focused, not value focused. There is a checklist of things to do and deliverables to produce. We do those things and produce those deliverables so that we can mark them off our list, whether or not they contribute to the success of the project or the quality of the outcome. We do them without even thinking about what we are doing. The daily stand-up will fill the time, whether there is anything meaningful to talk about or not. We will sit through a test scenario review meeting for two hours whether we can contribute meaningfully or not. We will produce the Functional Requirements document, even if the use cases that have already been created are infinitely more clear and all we need to move forward. We must check the box.

Good processes not only inform us of the steps that we need to take to reach the end, they promote and enable the qualities within our environment that we know are critical to achieving a successful outcome. To begin with, since the single most important characteristic for a successful outcome is the ability to learn, create, and innovate as a team, then first and foremost, a good process promotes and enables learning, creativity, and innovation. Humans, by nature, are highly adept at learning. We are inquisitive, curious, and possess tremendous brain power. We are also, by nature, highly creative. Not just some of us, all of us. Some of us are more predisposed to develop and use our creativity than others. Some of us are even determined to deny our creativity. But we are all creative, nonetheless.

If you don't believe me just take a moment and look around you: The plane in the sky, the buildings that surround you, the car you drive, the products that line your shelves, the devices you use in your daily life without even thinking — all the products of human creativity. The very act of shaping our lives is an act of creativity. Our ability to create is unlimited.

But there are also natural processes by which we learn and create. We study to acquire the basic concepts. We practice in order to develop deeper understanding and to train our minds and bodies in the mechanics. We learn by doing. We try, evaluate the results, adjust, and try again. This is how we learn to do everything: to walk, to paint, to play an instrument, to write poetry, to write software, to build systems.

The processes that we follow in the execution of transformational efforts should mirror our natural processes of learning and creation. Because every project is different and every situation is new, the need to learn along the way is inevitable. Since we learn the fastest by doing, our processes must support exactly that.

The principal reason that waterfall processes don't work is that they deny the natural processes of learning and creativity. We get exactly one shot at getting it right. All requirements must be known in advance (when there is no way we possibly can). They must be completed and signed off. Once they are signed off, they can't change. Once the design is complete and signed off, it can't change. When the code is being tested, everything we learn is a *defect,* not new knowledge or better understanding.

This causes us to do bad things. We can't get to the end of the requirements definition because we are terrified of missing something. We will include many requirements for functionality that we "may need," (though we probably won't) just to be safe. And yet, this will do nothing to ensure that we won't miss requirements for functionality that we do need, or those for functionality that we aren't yet aware we need.

Much later, during testing, we become litigators as we debate the interpretations of individual requirements; what was and was not in scope based on those interpretations; who was responsible for "missed" requirements. We desperately try to justify design choices after the fact, even if they were wrong. So much time and energy wasted on fear, simply because in a business setting, we can't emotionally come to grips with uncertainty, the need to learn, and the reality of the human process of learning. We think our risk is mitigated only by having all the answers up front, but it isn't. It can't be, because we can't know. Real leverage against the risk of uncertainty is not in pretending that there is certainty, but in being certain that we can and will learn.

This is why iterative processes on balance are far superior to waterfall processes. Much has been written on this topic, but the central premise is that we really know nothing for certain until we prove it. In other words, we won't know until we *try*. In general, the more chances we get to try, the faster we learn and the more likely we are to converge on a really good solution. Iterative processes, such as those in the family known as Agile Processes, have their weaknesses, but this isn't one of them. When it comes to acknowledging and embodying the reality of the human learning process, iterative processes are excellent.

By design, iterative processes give us the opportunity to learn by doing. They allow us many opportunities to learn and they formalize the process of incorporating what we learn back into the solution. We may struggle through the first iteration or two, but we soon pick up speed. This is far superior to struggling through the entire project. We discover errors in our thinking and errors in our solution early, while it is easy for us to adjust and adapt. This is far superior to discovering these things only after the entire solution is built and we are testing it for the first time. It allows us to be more creative and to take more risks with our ideas because be can prove them or disprove them quickly. The consequences for being wrong are not severe. As a result, the solutions that we ultimately invent are more innovative and more effective.

Since clarity is the minimum requirement for creativity and innovation, good processes promote clarity. Model-driven requirements analysis is one such process, but there are many others. For example, the design of the system must clearly describe *how* the requirements will be realized. There are better ways of doing this than others. The standard way is to fill out some sort of document template for the design. But document templates tend to be too detailed, too rigid, or both. Project teams have difficulty knowing what parts of a template to use and what to leave out. They feel compelled to complete them all even if the content is not useful in the given context. There may not be clear places for some of the details that are important to the design at hand. We will have to force these details into existing sections or add new sections. This is a time-consuming, inefficient process that forces us to make up a way to articulate our designs. And we have to do this every time. The variability from design to design is great. The variability in designs created by different people is even greater. This variability translates directly to lower quality and lower quality means problems down the road and higher costs.

A better way is model-driven design. First, it's a natural and seamless extension of model-driven requirements analysis. It is really just a matter of adding some additional design-related models: component models to express the architectural design, collaborations to express use case realizations, interactions, such as sequence diagrams and activity diagrams, to describe behavior. The requirements models translate easily to these design models. The correlation between the two is explicit and obvious. Therefore, the traceability from requirements to design is obvious. Better yet, this traceability is achieved with no extra effort. It is a natural by-product of the process. Finally, variability is greatly reduced, because model-driven design relies on standard modeling languages such as the UML to express design concepts in uniform ways that are widely understood and accepted.

During the construction phase, test-driven development is as much a tool for clarity as it is for verifying the software. The process calls for developers to write tests based on the requirements, preferably before even starting to write the software. This process causes a developer to become very clear about what the software he is about to write must do. Any ambiguity in the requirements, or anything missing, is immediately revealed and addressed. The tests themselves are better since they will reflect what the software is supposed to do rather than what it was built to do. These tests can then be automated and added to the suite of tests that the other developers are writing as they build their portions of the system. If we are confident in our requirements definition — and the tests are written against the requirements — when the automated tests are executed, we are absolutely clear at that moment about one very important thing: the software works, or it doesn't.

This is not trivial and its real value is not necessarily obvious. For example, it gives us incredible flexibility to make changes and to make them quickly as we learn. We can make a change, run the tests, and know immediately if the software works. If not, we know what else we need to change. During implementation, this allows us to make major revisions if necessary, even very late in the construction cycle. Over the life of the system, it gives us the freedom to advance the system as the needs of the business change, faster and without fear.

All of this results in built-in quality and less need for quality by inspection. When the relationship from requirements to design and from design to software is obvious, the uselessness of inspection becomes obvious. When we are confident that our tests reflect our requirements and when all our tests pass, we *know* the system works. For quality assurance I may want to sample some tests, particularly in high-risk areas, to be confident that the software is being properly tested, but I don't have to sit through hours of review sessions to review every single test. Later, during system test we can focus our efforts on the system as a whole and on more coverage for areas of high risk. In the end, we will test less and deliver the system sooner, while at the same time delivering much higher quality overall.

Good processes minimize non-value added effort. Non-value added effort is any activity that does not directly contribute to the creation of the solution. But don't misunderstand: non-value adding does not imply unimportant. It only means that it does not physically contribute to the asset itself. For example, inventing and designing the solution is value-adding. Writing software is value-adding. Unit testing in the development process is value-adding. All of these activities directly contribute to the asset itself. If you don't do these things, there is no asset.

On the other hand, a code review meeting is non-value adding. System testing is non-value adding. These activities verify the asset you have created, but they do not add to the asset. Again, this does not mean that they are unimportant. In fact, if your processes don't create good quality assets to begin with, then these activities are particularly critical. But the goal is to minimize these activities and to eliminate the unimportant non-value adding activities altogether.

Eliminating wasted effort is one thing, but even more leverage is achieved by reducing the effort required for value-adding activities. Good processes minimize manual effort. Anything that can be automated should be. Writing and maintaining documents is just that sort of effort. The real value is in the creation and innovation that results in the invention of the solution. The creation of project deliverables after the fact in order to demonstrate the work accomplished and to communicate the results to others is a ponderous, labor intensive effort. It tends to kill the momentum of the project while the team essentially stops in order to document what has been done. The results tend to be less than accurate, since as time passes after the moment of discovery and invention, knowledge dissipates. Details are lost since the effort required to capture them after the fact is often overwhelming.

Variability is also a problem. No two deliverables are the same from project to project. Team members spend enormous effort trying to figure out how to organize the content and communicate the information effectively. For all intents and purposes, project teams re-invent the project deliverables, as well as the process of creating them, on every project.

This is wildly inefficient and the results tend to be poor. Documents are thick but informationally shallow. They are full of boiler-plate content that is meaningless, and colorful, arbitrary works of art. They are poorly organized, badly written, and tedious to read. Their usefulness expires shortly after delivery, and they fill recycling bins to overflowing.

This is no excuse to abandon proper documentation. Just because it is done poorly does not mean it is unimportant. Proper documentation is critical. During the project, it is critical for crystallizing and communicating ideas. Over the course of time, it is critical to retaining knowledge and passing that knowledge on from team to team. It also saves significant amounts of cold hard cash: systems that are properly documented are more efficient to maintain and they have longer, useful lives.

Critics of documentation will say that this is only true if the documentation is up to date, and since it never is, it is useless. But again, just because it is done poorly does not mean it's unimportant. This is a problem of process, not a problem with documentation.

This is another area where model-driven processes shine. Documenting the models is part of the process of creating the models. Without the documentation, all you have are pictures, not models. But once the models are created and fully described, the documentation deliverables are simply a by-product. Creating up-to-date documentation is literally a matter of pushing a few buttons. Herein lies one of the most under-valued benefits of model-driven processes: by properly organizing the model of your solution, and by diligently describing and defining its components, you have created a proper outline for your deliverable, and you have written its content. And you have done it in the course of doing the heavy lifting of creation, innovation, and invention, which is the work that you have to do anyway. All that remains is to put a little thought into the order in which you want elements to appear in your documents, and you are finished.

This does not mean that it is effortless. Take note of the two very important preconditions that I just mentioned. The first is proper model organization. This is not a trivial task. It takes real thought and effort to organize your models in a way that reflects the design of your solution. Starting from an empty model project (the blank sheet of paper), the task of the project team is to invent the solution and to create models that reflect its design. Not just class models, but use case models and architecture models as well. You are literally creating a logical simulation of the system to be.

The second is that writing, and lots of it, is still required. You must write to describe the big ideas of your invention. You must write to explain aspects that are not intuitive. You must write to define the elements in the models: classes, attributes, operations, use cases, actors, packages, rules, activities, actions, etc. All of this writing needs to be done. But one of the great things about a model-driven process is that there are clear places within the models for all of it. All you have to do is fill in the details.

In a model-driven process, we use the activity of modeling to facilitate creation and invention. We use it to drive clarity, first for requirements, then for design. When the models are complete, the documentation is complete. Since I can generate my documentation deliverables from the models themselves, an enormous amount of manual effort is eliminated from the process. Finally, when my models are complete, I can push a button and *generate* a significant amount of the software that would otherwise have to be written by hand.

Why does any of this matter aside from simply trying to avoid work? The reason is simple: *productivity is king*. It wins over cost per hour every time. If one worker can produce twice as much in the same amount of time as another, that worker's effective hourly cost is half that of the other's. If you apply that to a team, it means that a team half the size can produce the same output in the same amount of time. Further, smaller teams are more productive than larger teams. They require less oversight and therefore bear less overhead. As team sizes scale, the productivity differential can grow to three to four times and even more. On a cost per hour basis, the more productive worker is now effectively one-quarter to one-third the cost of the less productive worker.

It may sound far-fetched, but we have seen far larger differentials. In one real-life situation, we replaced an existing team that had failed outright to deliver what they had promised. We had to scrap and rebuild everything they had "completed" and then deliver the rest. In the end, our team delivered in four months what a team *three times the size* couldn't deliver *in a year.*

This brings me to my final point: since quality and productivity go hand-in-hand, the less productive team will *never* produce a result equivalent to that of the more productive team. Not only will the productive team produce it faster and at a lower cost, the result will be better as well. This translates once again to cold hard cash. The higher-quality system will have a higher ROI, its cost of ownership will be lower, and its useful life will be longer. The bottom line is that IT organizations would have been far better served over the last decade pursuing productivity rather than chasing lower hourly rates and gutting their capabilities in the process.

11.
A PROCESS DISCIPLINE

There is good process and there is bad process, but *there is no such thing as no process*. To achieve a desired outcome, we must take a series of steps to perform some number of tasks. We can either take steps and perform tasks that we have deliberately and thoughtfully chosen to advance us toward our goal, or we can make it up as we go. In either case we are following some process. If we follow a process that has been developed based on experience and that is proven, the odds of achieving our desired outcome can be estimated. The better the process, the better our odds.

On the other hand, if we make the process up as we go, our chances of success are unknown. On average our outcomes will be worse and the variability in our outcomes will be broad. Variability equals uncertainty, and uncertainty equals risk. Once again, discipline in process is our weapon against uncertainty.

Imagine the result if a car manufacturer attempted to build each car of a particular model a little differently each time. Even a small change could have an enormous impact on productivity and quality. In a manufacturing scenario the effects of a lack of process discipline are obvious and immediate. In the field of IT, the effects are just as detrimental, but not nearly so obvious in the moment. There is typically some delay between cause and effect. Further, in manufacturing, it is actually fairly hard to buck the process, since it is enforced by the production line.

In our field there is no natural enforcement of process. Processes are enforced primarily through conscious effort and will. In many cases it is actually easier to not follow the process. This fact combined with the fact that the consequences of deviating from the process are not immediate and clear means that in the course of executing transformational efforts, we deviate from our processes more often than not. The impact on productivity should be obvious, but it isn't. Since the norm is to deviate from the process, the norm is low productivity. The impact on quality should be obvious, but it isn't. Again, the norm is that quality is low. Our experience has taught us what to expect. Until we experience something different, we don't know any better.

When we start a transformational effort, we begin with essentially nothing; what I like to call "The Blank Sheet of Paper." There are some ideas in people's heads. Sometimes they are more feelings than they are well-formed concepts. This is how all things, big or small, begin. We move from need or desire, to idea, to talk, to action. The first step, whether we want to take it or not, is to put the blank sheet of paper before us and to step into it. It is often a little overwhelming and a little deflating after all the energy and excitement around actually starting the project. It is kind of like standing at the base of Mount Everest, after all of the preparation, planning, and work to get there, when the grim reality of the magnitude of the task before us hits home. We can't even see the top of the mountain we face. It is obscured by the clouds of the unknown. The blank sheet of paper — how do we fill it? Like climbing the mountain, *one step at a time*.

The beauty and power of a process discipline, its magic simplicity, is this: if you take the steps that you know work, if you do those things, the page will be filled. You don't have to think about it.

You don't have to figure out what you are going to do *this time.* You already know. If you take the steps, the page *will be filled.* The requirements will become clear, the solution will be invented, it will be built, and it will be implemented. You will look down from the top of the mountain and say, "Wow. Look how far we have come."

But here is the catch. You must take those steps and do those things that are proven to work, and you must be *uncompromising* and *relentless.* This means that you must hold before you at all times the vision of a successful outcome, not just for you, but for everyone. You will not simply follow the rules, you will own the game. You will learn to say 'no,' and you will say it as often as necessary. The inevitable pressures will arise. The requirements definition is taking longer than planned and the project manager is pressuring you to just call it complete. You say, "No." You have provided your best estimate for accomplishing some task, and you are getting pressure to commit to getting it done sooner. You say, "No." Someone doesn't like your model-driven process and you are pressured to produce your requirements a different way. You say, "No." Someone thinks that the deliverables you produce are too heavy and not "Agile enough." Someone thinks your deliverables are inadequate because they can't check all the boxes on their pre-defined list. They all want you to do something different. You say, "No. No. No."

Discipline in process means that you resist non-value-added effort. It means that when you know a shifting-the-burden event is occurring, you speak up. It means that when you see that a standard and accepted practice that everyone is blindly following is self-defeating, you speak up. It means that you make every effort to help and to teach. If your help and guidance is welcomed, great. If it is met with resistance, you may have to back off. But under no circumstances do you erode what you do simply to make someone else more comfortable.

Does this sound harsh and unyielding? Does it sound aloof and arrogant? You will be accused of these things and more. You will be told that it is more important to be a 'team player.' You will be called pedantic, impractical, unreasonable. People will be angry with you. You will be in trouble often. My personal favorite: "The trouble with those guys is that it's their way or the highway." That pretty much sums it up.

This is why it's called a *discipline*. Like climbing Everest, it's not easy. Despite your preparation, your training, your experience, and your knowledge; despite the fact that the route up the mountain is clear to you — it is still difficult. The one thing that you can control is what *you* do: the actions you take, how you respond to pressure, how you react to the circumstances. Discipline in process means that you acknowledge what you control and you own it. You don't relinquish it to anyone for any reason.

There are plenty of things that we can't control. Climbing Everest, we can't control the weather, snow conditions, illness. Climbing our mountain, we can't control politics, changes in funding, economic conditions, and a myriad of other factors. This is why success is never guaranteed, and why it is so critical to control what we can, despite the difficulty.

I know this sounds contentious. Sometimes it is. We are, after all, not doing easy things. But in far more than equal measures you will also experience more success. You will earn more respect. You will make great friends. And you will do more good. These are the rewards of being disciplined.

Finally, process discipline provides a baseline for continuous improvement. If we are disciplined we can see what is working and what needs to be improved. We can improve our processes deliberately over time. It is a good first step to define a process and then to follow it, but it is not enough. To be disciplined in process also means being disciplined about making the processes better. Continuous improvement is *mandatory*.

In the field of information technology, continuous improvement is all but a lost concept. To continuously improve, you must first define and then strictly follow a process. Since our processes are constantly changing as we constantly deviate, we can't even begin to improve them. We have no predictability. One project is successful. We are happy. The next project is a failure. We are sad. Both results are essentially accidents. But once we are disciplined, we can change that. Not because discipline automatically makes our processes better, but because it enables us to evaluate their effectiveness. And as we do, our predictability and certainty improves, our variability in results is reduced, our quality improves, and our productivity increases. This is how success over the long-haul is measured.

My intention is not to prescribe for you a particular process or methodology. That is the subject of another book. My intention is only to lay out for you the principles that you can use as a guide for developing and evaluating your own processes. People often ask me what methodology we follow. The answer is "our own." By now, you have probably guessed that I prefer model-driven, iterative processes. I am a fan of anything that promotes learning, creativity, and clarity. I am looking for anything and everything that will drive out waste, improve our productivity, and improve our quality. Over the years I have made serious attempts to adopt methodologies that I thought held promise. After all, why reinvent the wheel? In the end they all fell short in one way or another, however, each and every one had their strengths. We have adopted the best aspects of them all and left the rest by the roadside.

Our "methodology," if we are to call it that, is an amalgamation of many others with a sprinkling of new things that the others lacked. Model-driven methods are exceptional for promoting clarity and driving the process of invention. Agile methods are excellent at promoting collaboration and communication and are the best thing going today in the area of project planning and tracking. Iterative methods as a category are excellent in that they promote learning by doing. Even waterfall methods, despite their fatal flaws, are good about making us use our heads and *think* before we just dive in and start building stuff. The point is, for those of us who are into this sort of thing, it doesn't matter what we label it. It only matters what we accomplish with it. We tend to get hung up on the labels: it's bad to be waterfall; it's cool to be Agile. The only thing that matters is results.

PARTING THOUGHTS

"A discipline converts a 'craft' into a methodology – such as engineering, the scientific method, the quantitative method or the physician's differential diagnosis. Each of these methodologies converts ad hoc experience into system. Each converts anecdote into information. Each converts skill into something that can be taught and learned."

PETER F. DRUCKER [1]

In his 1992 book, *Post-Capitalist Society*, Peter F. Drucker observed that, "The basic economic resource – 'the means of production' to use the economist's term – is no longer capital, nor natural resources (the economist's 'land'), nor 'labour'. *It is and will be knowledge.*"[2] Drucker was describing the transformational shift away from an economy where capital and labor were the driving forces to one where the specialized knowledge and skills held in the heads of the *knowledge-worker* had become "…the real and controlling resource and the absolutely decisive 'factor of production.'"[3] He went on to say that, "Value is now created by 'productivity' and 'innovation', both applications of knowledge to work."[4]

The "new technologies" of the Industrial Revolution were, among other things, the steam engine and mass-production, which leveraged capital to build plants and machines and labor to work in them and run them. Many of the standard practices that we continue to apply to this day in the course of dispatching transformational efforts, particularly in the area of project management, are left over from the days of the Industrial Revolution and the "productivity revolution"[6] that followed. They are all about leveraging labor. We manage tasks. We manage time. We give little real thought or effort to the factors that actually create value in our knowledge-based economy — creativity and innovation. As I have said before, transformational efforts suffer at the hands of traditional, linear, command and control project management. Any knowledge-based activity will.

The "new technologies" of our modern economy are those required to leverage knowledge for creativity and "Systematic Innovation."[5] These technologies or *disciplines* are the disciplines of trust, the discipline of clarity, and the discipline of process. As creativity and innovation become increasingly vital to value creation, effectively leveraging the brain power and inherent creativity of people will become paramount. In fact, it already has. "Effectively" means productively, repeatably, and predictably. Though the focus of this book is primarily on the area of information technology, these principles apply to any knowledge-based activity where groups of highly-specialized and knowledgeable individuals must collaborate effectively to *invent*.

Clarity is the minimum requirement for creativity and innovation. Clarity in this sense is not just the acquisition of knowledge, but also discovery, synthesis, common understanding, and the emergence of entirely new ideas; the essence of innovation itself. A *discipline* of clarity is the body of theory and technique that must be studied, mastered, and put into practice to leverage the knowledge of a group of specialists to achieve clarity in a repeatable, predictable, and productive way.

Clarity depends heavily on trust. Our day-to-day reality is one where we each bring our specialized knowledge to a situation, and must interact and collaborate with each other in a highly personal, often intense, and even intimate way. It's not that we have to be best friends, but it is mandatory that we *trust* each other. It is impossible to achieve clarity in a low-trust environment. A *discipline* of trust is the body of theory and technique that we put into practice to build an *operational trust* [7] in a repeatable, predictable way.

Predictability, repeatability, and most importantly, productivity depend on process. A *discipline* of process means putting in place processes that are proven to work and having the discipline to follow them *relentlessly*. Good processes not only inform us of the steps that we need to take to reach the end, they promote and enable the qualities within our environment that we know are critical to achieving a successful outcome. They promote learning and creativity; they promote clarity; they minimize non value-added effort. Finally, to be disciplined in process also means being disciplined about making the processes better. Continuous improvement is *mandatory*.

I wish I could say that it is easy; that it is simply a matter of mechanics. Just follow the steps. There are mechanics, of course, and there are steps. There are even steps that you can take right now. But it is more than just going through the motions. These three disciplines describe a "new technology" for leveraging knowledge. And they also describe the requirements and characteristics of *being disciplined*. This aspect is more about changing our hearts and minds, and *that* is the hard part, because it requires us to examine ourselves. It requires that we recognize that *we* are our own worst enemies and to change the behaviors that undermine ourselves and each other. It requires us to be more vulnerable and to take more risks, especially with each other, but it is mandatory that we do this. If any of us is to remain competitive and succeed in an increasingly competitive global economy, we have to get really good at creating and innovating on-demand and predictably, not just in the field of information technology, but in every field: marketing, finance, product development, manufacturing, logistics, you name it. We face big challenges socially, environmentally, economically, and politically. Across the board, we need to learn to bring to bear our massive collective creative ability in order to create and invent solutions to these challenges. The field of information technology is as good a place as any to start. After all, information technology is pervasive, and plays an increasingly central and vital role in all aspects of business and government.

Notes

1. Drucker, Peter F. *Post-Capitalist Society*. New York: Routledge, 2011. iBooks. https://itun.es/us/LRBnH.l. p.107

2. ibid., p. 31

3. ibid., p. 28

4. ibid., p. 32

5. ibid., p. 98

6. ibid., p. 53-64

7. Senge, Peter M. *The Fifth Discipline: The Art and Practice of the Learning Organization*. Rev. and updated. ed. New York: Doubleday/Currency, 2006. p. 219.

BIBLIOGRAPHY

Collins, Jim. *Good to Great: Why Some Companies Make the Leap...
And Others Don't* HarperBusiness, 2011. iBooks. https://itun.es/us/
yhVOA.l.

Covey, Stephen R. *The 7 Habits of Highly Successful People.* 25th
Anniversary Edition: RosettaBooks LLC, 2013.

Deming, W. Edwards. *Out of the Crisis.* Cambridge, Mass.:
Massachusetts Institute of Technology, Center for Advanced
Engineering Study, 1986.

Deming, W. Edwards. *The New Economics for Industry, Government,
Education.* Cambridge, MA: Massachusetts Institute of Technology,
Center for Advanced Engineering Study, 1993.

Drucker, Peter F. *Post-Capitalist Society.* New York: Routledge, 2011.
iBooks. https://itun.es/us/LRBnH.l.

Lencioni, Patrick. *Getting Naked: A Business Fable About Shedding
the Three Fears That Sabotage Client Loyalty.* San Francisco, CA:
Jossey-Bass, 2010.

Porter, Michael E. "Strategy and the Internet." *Harvard Business Review OnPoint*, 2001.

Porter, Michael E. "What Is Strategy?" *Harvard Business Review*, November-December 1996.

Schön, Donald A. *The Reflective Practitioner: How Professionals Think in Action*. New York: Basic Books, 1983.

Senge, Peter M. *The Fifth Discipline: The Art and Practice of the Learning Organization*. Rev. and updated ed. New York: Doubleday/Currency, 2006.

The Standish Group. *The Chaos Manifesto*. The Standish Group International, 2009. Professional report, self-published.

Evans, Eric. *Domain-Driven Design: Tackling Complexity in the Heart of Software*: Addison-Wesley, 2003.

ACKNOWLEDGMENTS

First, I want to thank my wife, Sherry, for her infinite patience, loving support, and for the countless hours just listening as she weathered my many ups and downs over the years that it took to produce this book. She deserves a medal, probably the Purple Heart.

I am deeply grateful to the giants on whose shoulders I stand, Peter M. Senge, W. Edwards Deming, Peter F. Drucker, Jim Collins, Michael E. Porter, and others. These are the Great Ones, and I am truly indebted to them.

Thanks to my cousin and business partner, Tom Wilger, and to my brilliant TEKNOVARE team members whom I have diabolically conscripted as my primary test subjects. I am truly blessed to work with such amazing people. Thanks to our many clients from whom I learned so much. In particular, I want to thank Sean Bristol, Bob Melkerson, and John Jankowski (whom we lost along the way) for their incredible support, participation, and patience as we developed our technique over the years. Thanks to Jason Pengelly for the many conversations and profound insights.

Thanks to Kevin W. Hartley for his mentorship over the years, and for seeing something in a young, scared, lost kid that I couldn't see in myself. Finally, thanks to Royce M. Palazzo for getting it all started so many years ago.

Printed in the United States
By Bookmasters